David T. Mason: Forestry Advocate

DAVID T. MASON
Forestry Advocate

His Role in the Application of Sustained Yield
Management to Private and Public Forest Lands

Elmo Richardson

Forest History Society, Inc.
Santa Cruz, California

The Forest History Society is a nonprofit, educational institution dedicated to the advancement of historical understanding of man's interaction with the North American forest environment. It was established in 1946. Interpretations and conclusions in publications prepared by the Forest History Society are those of the authors; the Society takes responsibility for the selection of topics, the competence of the authors, and their freedom of inquiry.

Work on this book and its publication were supported by grants to the Forest History Society.

Library of Congress Cataloging in Publication Data
Richardson, Elmo.
    David T. Mason, forestry advocate.

    Bibliography: p.
    Includes index.
    1. Mason, David Townsend, 1883-1973. 2. Foresters—United States Biography. 3. Forest management—United States—History. I. Forest History Society. II. Title. III. Title: Sustained yield management to private and public forest lands.
    SD129.M3R53   1983   634.9'092'4 [B]   83-16533
    ISBN 0-89030-044-5

In Memory Of
Max Savelle and Herman Deutsch
Brave, Gentle Knights
Who Believed That
Teaching Is The Noblest Profession

Contents

Introduction

David Townsend Mason was a numbers-counter, one of an impressively small company of early-day quantifiers. The years of his long life (1883-1973) coincided with a period when these inventors and engineers, these corporate and political empire-builders, assumed direction of the nation's progress by measuring and managing natural and human resources. Writing and speaking the language of computation long before the age of electronic computers, they calculated yields per acre, gallons per minute and per mile, production volumes per operation per day, demographic concentrations and shifts.

Most importantly they recognized that their theories and findings had to be applied by government as well as private enterprise. A few of them were able to use the leverages of wealth or personal power. But others wielded great influence as colleagues, committeemen, and consultants. Mason was one of these. He was the honest broker, bringing together diverse and often antagonistic interests to find mutual advantages. He bridged what in his time was an enormous gap between private interests and the public interest. Yet he thought of himself as a crusader. After constructing the first integrated model for sustained-yield forest management, he led the movement for its adoption by government and by a doubting, depressed lumber industry.

Sustained-yield forest management was a timely idea when Mason arrived on the scene. Regulation of forest use had been a necessity in western Europe since the thirteenth century. Thereafter, demand by expanding national states for such raw materials facilitated formulation of managerial methodologies. During the Age of Enlightenment, new mathematics and sciences produced the principles incorporated into the economic philosophy of commercial capitalism. Wood-based construction soon gave way to iron and steel, but timber productivity remained a vital development even in industrialized nations like Germany and France, where quantifiers devised formulae for control of that productivity.

At the end of the nineteenth century, American foresters began analyzing the applicability of these European techniques to distinctly different conditions in their nation's relatively abundant timber tracts. Lumbermen agreed that some of these theories were impressive, but others were too rigid or costly. Protection of standing timber and planned control of annual production seemed far more practical than the selective logging of forests containing a variety of timber types and ages. For another decade, the subject of practical forest management seemed purely academic. After 1912 a few government bodies, such as the Oregon State Board of Forestry, set aside public tracts for growth and harvesting experiments, while one or two lumber companies included selective logging in their schedules. For about six years—1918 to 1924—an industry blessed with an increasing market for accessible timber on privately owned lands generally ignored foresters' discussions of means for sustaining lumber production. But when their prosperity was shaken by larger economic developments, theories and experiments took on immediate significance.

Because David Mason emphasized the "capital efficiency" of scientific management, he appealed to a wider spectrum of forest owners than did the academics. Familiar with the forestry techniques analyzed and debated by his elders, he pointed to the factor that underlay all of them: annual allowable cut. While including protection, production control, and selective logging in his plan to sustain yields, he emphasized that cut was the primary balance weight for determining every other aspect of productive capacity and capital value.[1]

One of Mason's well-wishers called him the "Johnny Appleseed" of sustained yield.[2] The image does not exactly fit the facts. The proselytizer was never a lone figure traveling through an unpopulated landscape of opportunity. He was still a "greenhorn" forestry student in 1907 when Charles S. Chapman was investigating the possibilities of selective cutting in the southern pine region. A decade later, he was just one of several imaginative academics and thereafter one of many idea men in the field offices of the lumber industry and the anterooms of government. Even though these advocates of forest management were associates, they devoted a good portion of their efforts to defending their own version of the concept from the ambitions of each other. Three of the most prominent were Edward T. Allen of the Western Forestry and Conservation Association, who did not hide his continuing hostility toward Mason; William B. Greeley of the West Coast Lumbermen's Association, who gave no more than a passing nod to Mason in his autobiography, *Forests and Men*; and Wilson M. Compton of the National Lumber Manufacturers' Association, who later summed up Mason's role as "not much."[3] Like many other movements in human history, adoption of sustained-yield forestry was clearly the result of intramural rivalries. But achievement was determined not so much by power as by persistence and presence, two of Mason's strongest attributes.

Nor did he indiscriminately scatter the seeds of his cause or expect them to grow unattended. With a keen perception for the right moment, and for his associates' reasoning, he gradually cultivated receptive ground by calculating the probable limits of effectiveness. Moreover, he well understood the impressiveness of practical, profitable results. It may be said that his own performance started with a paper that served as a veritable "Common Sense" in the revolution of the nation's lumber economy.

While others were preoccupied with symptoms and partial cures of the industry's chronic ills, Mason projected sustained yield's maximum feasible impact. With the firm conviction that capitalism and democracy could be yoked together without resort to compulsion, he proposed a set of scientifically sound priorities that were applicable to the basic problems of economic depressions as well as prosperities. To a great extent, he devoted his consulting business to showing lumbermen how they could engineer their own salvation. Drawing upon the results of these initial experiments, he quickly expanded his campaign just when trade organizations and government departments at several levels were searching for solutions to market instabilities in the face of growing scarcity of accessible timber resources. In doing so, his Yale classmate Thornton T. Munger judged, Mason succeeded in accomplishing a task that the forestry profession should have completed twenty years earlier.[4]

The voluntarism underlying his proposals interested the Herbert Hoover administration and the First New Deal of Franklin D. Roosevelt. At the same time, Mason's emphasis on executive planning and statutory mandate reassured lumbermen. From the viewpoint of the latter, however, federal timidity was followed by a period of federal heavy-handedness. As overseer of the Lumber Code Authority under the National Recovery Administration (NRA), Mason shared lumbermen's bitter conclusion that the New Dealers meant to use the emergency conditions to maneuver the industry into a position of subservience to bureaucratic regulation in order to establish federal control of the forest economy.

In the years following the Supreme Court's invalidation of the NRA, Mason helped to reconcile the apparent antagonisms of industrial self-government and government management. Sustained yield, he argued, could be practiced on selected public and private forest tracts under mutually agreeable contract terms. These cooperative sustained-yield units were authorized by legislation for which he was a prime mover: the Oregon and California Revested Lands Act of 1937 and the Sustained-Yield Forest Management Act of 1944. Thereafter, the old specters of compulsion and centralism—periodically inflated by economic hubris and political controversy—truncated the potential application of cooperative management. But these statutes still serve as yardsticks for a less rigidly structured policy applied to forest properties throughout the nation.

Mason's second legacy was also based upon his ubiquitous presence in the eye of many storms. He knew as colleagues, friends, and rivals most of the men who dominated the lumber economy for over sixty years. At the urging of Elwood R. Maunder, executive director of the Forest History Society, his voluminous papers were housed at the Oregon Historical Society in Portland. For historians, they are a treasure trove not only of natural resource development but also of the interaction of private and public sectors of the nation's economy. Mason shared his generation's belief that the best kind of conservation was that which brought sustained profit. As these records show, his work for clients reconciled conservation and development. Thousands of folders of correspondence, documents, statistics, and proposals delineate the physical and financial conditions involved in harmonizing those programs.

The present study is, of course, a summary account of the one theme that preoccupied Mason; it is only an episode in the complex events of forest history. But it points to several significant subjects that must be examined far more extensively: the development of lumber trade associations, the influence of foresters' organizations, the interaction between the industry and government at every level, and the changing pattern of forestland ownership, use, and productivity. This account admittedly emphasizes Mason's abilities—those attributes that enabled him to accomplish his good work. Modesty must not get in the way of justifiable pride. Near the end of his life, he once threw that quality "to the winds" by saying, "I developed the idea [of sustained yield] . . . in a comparatively short time."[5] The adjective was revealing: in the world of foresters and lumbermen, the measure of time spans the many decades it takes for a tree to grow from seed to forest giant.

The author gladly acknowledges the men and women who gave personal testimony about Mason and the lumber industry, and in other ways helped in the preparation of this text. Harold "Pete" Steen, executive director of the Forest History Society, thoughtfully brought the assignment to me, and the Northwest Area Foundation generously sustained the major cost of the research, writing, and publication. Financial support was also received from the Grotto Foundation, and Gilbert M. Bowe, Carl A. Newport, and Glenn A. Zane of Mason,

Bruce & Girard, Inc. Judy Reardon and Larry Myers, trusty helpers of another year, examined collections at Washington, D.C., New Haven, Connecticut, and Hyde Park, New York, and provided me with the results of their perceptive searches; the staffs of several manuscript and archive depositories were invariably helpful in my own digging. I am grateful for the special arrangements granted by Thomas Vaughan, director of the Oregon Historical Society. The successive curators of that depository's Manuscripts Division, Cathy DeLorge and Steven Hallberg, facilitated and brightened the work there considerably. I appreciate the scrutiny given the manuscript by Gilbert M. Bowe, Robert W. Cowlin, William D. Hagenstein, Rodney C. Loehr, Elwood R. Maunder, William G. Robbins, Richard F. Smith, and Harold K. Steen; the book is undoubtedly better as a result of their comments. Without my leaning over her shoulder, Ann Bennett carefully typed the very messy pages of two submittal versions; she has my admiration and gratitude.

Elmo Richardson

David T. Mason:
Forestry Advocate

1

The Compleat Forester

David T. Mason was born in Newark, New Jersey, and grew up in Bound Brook, a community of about 1,500 people located in the state's still-wooded northeastern section. His father, William Mason, owned, published, proofread, and did most of the reporting for the town's weekly newspaper, the *Chronicle*. He was also the postmaster, organizer of a bank, and manager of a water utility. A "sparkplug" of civic progress, in his son's admiring phrase, he declined the powers of political office, preferring to work as an equal with those whose help he needed to accomplish a variety of projects.

David's mother, born Rachel Townsend in nearby Paterson, was as even tempered, well informed, and gregarious as her husband. While pursuing one of her favorite recreations, botanizing, she often took her children on walks to a nearby rocky promontory called Stone Crop, site of a skirmish between George Washington's men and British troops during the Revolution. From the stories she and other relatives told, David learned that his ancestors had been craftsmen and small business-men in New England and New York since the mid-seventeenth century. But history was also an ongoing thing for him. As a boy, he saw the "dappled" glow produced by Newark's electric light system—the invention of the city's neighbor, Thomas Edison—and he rode a new technological marvel, the interurban train, to attend high school in Paterson.[1]

Mason worked as printer's devil and reporter on the *Chronicle*, pruned trees, and helped survey the town's water pipelines. At school his first love was baseball, and it would always remain close to his heart. But he also valued the time spent studying Latin because it enabled him to use the English language with precision. When he finished high school, he joined the student body of 250 at Rutgers University, only a few miles from his home. He was an eager participant in three sports there, yet found time to major in civil engineering, partly because that

3

profession would keep him in the great outdoors that he enjoyed so much. Although he earned Phi Beta Kappa honors, he never considered himself a good scholar. With similar modesty, he usually ascribed each gratifying turn in his life to "a stroke of good luck."

Sometime in the course of his undergraduate years, Mason experienced a kind of inspiration. Sitting atop Stone Crop at sunset one day, he had a feeling that he "did want to do some good in the world." Later, when his mother called his attention to the profession of forestry, he recognized that civil engineering would be a useful foundation for the management aspect of that field.[2]

In 1905 young Mason applied for admission at Yale University, which he knew was "a great athletic college." More importantly it had the best of the three schools of forestry in the nation at that time. Gifford Pinchot, chief forester of the recently reorganized U. S. Forest Service in the Department of Agriculture, was one of the university's best-known alumni. Determined to build a strong administration, Pinchot proposed to apply to the millions of acres of national forests under his agency's jurisdiction a program of long-term, multiple-purpose management—"conservation," as it would soon be called. Mason was one of the handful of self-confident forestry students at Yale who hoped to join in Pinchot's crusade for scientific forestry. In preparation for their career, they studied silviculture, a science that was still new in the curricula of American colleges. Combining the fundamentals of botany, geography, and mathematics, it was designed to gauge and predict forest growth. Among the teachers the young men proudly "broke in" were those they called "Gravy" (Dean Henry S. Graves) and "Chappie" (Herman H. Chapman). Carl A. Schenck was one of the visiting lecturers who explained to them cutting practices that had sustained forests in Europe throughout centuries of war and population movements.

Except for Sir William Schlich's *Manual of Forestry* (1903), there were no texts on forest management theories available in English. Instead, the class learned the practical bases for such procedures by doing summer fieldwork. Because one of their camps was located in northwestern New Jersey, just across the Delaware River from Pinchot's home at Milford, Pennsylvania, the young men's idol sometimes visited their campfire to give them spirited talks. Mason wrote up an account of one such experience, and his father proudly printed it in the *Chronicle*. During another field trip to Grandin, in the Missouri Ozarks, the fledgling forester began to record his ongoing activities, essentially as a sequence of meetings with various people. That diary became the first of more than sixty volumes, one for each year of his long life.[3]

Among those who graduated with him in 1907 were men whose names later became notable in the annals of the profession: Samuel T. Dana would build up the University of Michigan's forestry school; Hugo Winkenwerder would do the same at the University of Washington; Ovid M. Butler would become executive secretary of the American Forestry Association (AFA); Charles S. Judd, scion of the pioneer Hawaiian missionary family, became the islands' first chief forester; Harvey R. MacMillan would hold that position in British Columbia and later organize the B. C. lumber company, MacMillan Bloedel Limited. The road to such accomplishments, however, would be a long one. Some members of the class began by working for lumber companies. Because those enterprises were not then concerned with forest management, more idealistic graduates looked to the Forest Service. With Chapman's recommendation, Mason was one of several who took the federal civil service examination and was duly accepted at the agency's headquarters in Washington, D.C.

His first assignment was to the secretarial pool known as the Bull Pen. There, he was impressed by Pinchot's demand for clear and precise syntax and was delighted when the chief approved his drafts without further editing. The members of the close-knit Society of American Foresters (SAF)—known as the Baked Apple Club when it met at Pinchot's home—soon took him into their company and thereby laid the foundation for his subsequent network of influential friendships. After several months as clerk, Mason may have despaired of ever seeing a forest. But his immediate superior, Earle H. Clapp, promised to take him west and "drop" him on a national forest. Mason's first landing place was the Montezuma National Forest in southwestern Colorado.

To the stockmen, miners, and lumbermen of that last fragment of the frontier, what they called Pinchotism was already anathema. The new ranger, with his sleeping bag from Abercrombie & Fitch and a noticeable inability to stay on a horse for long, hardly allayed their hostility. One local forest user was soon complaining to his senator about "a youngster that hasn't got any whiskers" who accused him "over and over again" of being a trespasser on the public reserve. Pinchot, of course, considered that charge high praise for his ranger. In time, however, Mason recognized that lumbermen often resorted to illegal or wasteful practices because of inaccurate, vague, and inadequate government regulations and statutes. As a result, he developed a particular interest in making surveys and analyses that could be used to correct those conditions. On subsequent timber cruising assignments, he worked on the Coeur d'Alene (Idaho) and Olympic (Washington) national forests. Many forest owners he observed there believed that taxes levied by counties, as if timber was a nonrenewable resource, pared away their profits and thus made them all the more anxious to liquidate their holdings as quickly as possible. Although studies then and thereafter indicated no such relationship between taxes and profits, there seemed to be a particularly dismaying circle of cause and effect. Such behavior in turn accounted for counties' assumptions and foresters' criticism.[4]

In 1908 Mason joined the Forest Service's newly established District One, with headquarters in Missoula, Montana. William B. Greeley was its chief; his assistant was Ferdinand A. Silcox. The newcomer's immediate superior was Albert W. Cooper, director of the silvicultural section. The work they did further reinforced Mason's solicitude for lumbermen. Cooper taught him to take into account all economic factors affecting company bids for federal timber. He was dismayed to find, however, that the agency would not make allowance for defective stumpage in its measurement of volume in sales. Aware that Pinchot desired to make the Forest Service independent of congressional appropriations by increasing sales, Cooper and Mason noted that actual transactions fell far short of possible totals in District One, which brought in about 40 percent of the revenue from logging in the national forest system. When they brought such questions to the attention of their colleague, Greeley evidently rejected their arguments. These disagreements may have accounted for Cooper's resignation soon after. Moreover, Mason felt that he was passed over for Cooper's vacated post, which was given to Robert Y. Stuart, who, as with Greeley and Silcox, was a future chief of the Forest Service.[5]

Wisely concluding that it would be "a damned good thing" if he had a national forest of his own to supervise, Mason gladly accepted the next opening, Deerlodge National Forest near Anaconda, Montana. In those halcyon days, a supervisor largely improvised, basing his decisions on the few regulations contained in the small manual called the *Use Book*. To provide a sounder basis for judgment, Mason initiated a study of regeneration in the lodgepole pine that was indigenous to the area. The Anaconda Mining Company, which dominated the area's economy, held as much pine land as the government—a million acres—but was also a large purchaser of federal timber. Because sulphur and arsenic fumes from Anaconda's mills killed timber over great swaths of the surrounding forests, Mason tried to find techniques that might facilitate regeneration. From a correspondence course he was taking in the efficiency concepts of Frederick W. Taylor, and from the Franklin Automobile Company's practice of time-and-motion production, he learned how to greatly increase the planting of seedlings in cutover or damaged areas. His project, which involved setting aside acreage for experimental tracts and assigning assistant rangers to gather data, had

Silcox's support. Greeley was also interested in measurement methodology, but after the company objected to inclusion of replanting requirements in the sales contracts, he expressed objections to Mason's work, ostensibly because of the time and personnel the study required. The experiments nevertheless gave Mason practical examples that he used in lectures to classes at the nearby University of Montana and back at Yale during the winter seasons.[6]

In 1912 he succeeded Stuart as assistant district forester. His paramount concern in that office was fire protection. Between 1910 and 1914, holocausts killed billions of board feet of timber in the adjacent areas of Washington, Idaho, and Montana known as the Inland Empire. Because private and state lands were intermingled with the national forests, fire-fighting crews included both lumber company employees and government rangers. The strategy and tactics they used—and the funds to support them—perforce depended upon mutual consultation and cooperation. Setting an example, Mason and his rangers worked on the fire line with volunteers. While on that duty, he was impressed with initiatives taken by several lumbermen to organize and sustain fire-protection associations.[7] Among these were the directors of the Weyerhaeuser Timber Company, with extensive holdings in the Pacific Northwest. In programs for their own lands and through membership in forest owner and lumber manufacturing associations, Weyerhaeuser also promoted state legislation for ongoing, broad-based cooperation.[8] As these businessmen saw it, timber value was fundamental to the problem of forest practices. That same relationship particularly interested Mason.

Since 1899 Pinchot had offered a program of information and assistance to lumbermen on a cooperative contract basis. The response was enthusiastic. Partly in reaction to the enlargement of federal forestlands, members of the lumber industry had already begun to organize to assert their own interests and to protect their public image. For example, the Western Forestry and Conservation Association (WFCA) was established in Spokane, Washington, in 1909, primarily as a clearinghouse for information to be considered by industry and government. Edward T. Allen, a former California and federal forester who founded the WFCA, assured federal officials of the industry's interest in permanent forest management. Allen's colleague, George S. Long, Weyerhaeuser's manager for West Coast operations, urged lumbermen to implement a concept that would soon be widely referred to as industrial self-government. But conservative and individualistic lumbermen seemed unwilling or unable to support joint efforts to regulate production or overproduction. Moreover, because cooperative organizations were in fact trade associations, they were in possible violation of federal antitrust acts. Henry Graves, by then Pinchot's successor as chief of the Forest Service, had revived his predecessor's idea of securing legislation that would exempt forest management cooperatives from that law.[9]

In 1914 the Bureau of Corporations questioned the motives of lumbermen's associations when it charged that some impeded collection of the newly levied federal corporation tax by manipulating market prices to control timber production. The Forest Service hoped to remain neutral in the matter yet provide some assistance to both parties. It therefore initiated studies of ownership patterns throughout the national forest regions. Because of Mason's experience, he was asked to write the report for the Inland Empire. As a beginning, he brought several young rangers to his office as assistants, including Donald Bruce and Emanuel Fritz. Mason also wrote a study of field reconnaissance procedures, aided by another ranger in his district, James W. Girard, and completed a study of lodgepole pine that became a standard text for forestry schools and the Forest Service.[10]

Mason's written work impressed a new friend and an old one. Wilson Compton, working on a graduate degree in economics, came out from New York to discuss with him the theory and practice of forest management. Professor Chapman, meanwhile, recommended Mason for a place on the faculty of the University of California's new Division of Forestry. The salary was to be $2,800—a convincing contrast to the $1,800 he was earning after seven years with the Forest Service. By now a married man (Evelyn Polleys, who became his wife in 1911, was the daughter of a prominent Missoula lumberman) with a college loan to pay off, Mason accepted the position with enthusiasm. Some of his colleagues showed the darker side to their famous camaraderie by considering his decision to leave the Forest Service as a matter of deserting ship. Although he had not wholly blackened his name (as they felt others were doing) by going to work for men whom they thought of as "timber devastators," they viewed him with some suspicion.

In the fall of 1915, Mason was delighted to move from Montana's snows to the balmy weather of California, where he could work and play outdoors all year round. He found the academic climate at Berkeley equally comfortable. His superiors supported his research by allowing him to devote halftime to the still-unfinished Inland Empire report. The other half of his work consisted of lecturing to small classes of would-be foresters. He taught them his special interest: the finance and administration of commercial forests. With evident satisfaction, he noted in his diary that one course, entitled "The Lumber Industry," drew fifty students, while others, "including two women," had to be turned away. But he was shocked by the poor quality of writing on examination papers and soon headed a committee that recommended English proficiency be added to the college's curriculum requirements.

The entries in his diaries for these years indicate that Mason had many other interests in addition to his teaching. He immediately began meeting with the most prominent lumbermen and foresters of the state and with those coming into the area for a variety of conventions and special projects. He also wrote several articles suggesting forestry programs at the state level and urging changes in format and content for the SAF's publication, which in 1917 became the *Journal of Forestry*.[11]

When the nation began its preparedness program in 1916, he was one of twelve faculty members who joined in community drill exercises. After the declaration of war in April 1917, Graves secured a captain's commission for him in the newly formed Tenth Engineers Regiment-Forestry. Granted leave by the university, Mason helped plan equipment supplies for the unit as it assembled in Washington, D.C. Later, he accompanied it to Britain and then to Bordeaux, located in the pine region of southwestern France. There the Tenth Engineers directed logging and lumber stockpiling operations that proceeded with such speed that the scheduled production rates were surpassed in less than a year. Mason noted, however, that French foresters considered American methods wasteful. Unable to obtain a front-line assignment, he returned to Washington, D.C., to train candidates for another regiment. The war's end put a halt to that program, and Mason was discharged with the rank of major, a title he proudly continued to use.[12]

He was back at Berkeley for only a few months when he again applied for leave to respond to another instance of "terrific good luck." Compton, now executive secretary of the National Lumber Manufacturers Association (NLMA), and E. T. Allen, who held a similar post in the WFCA, had spoken with Mason while he was in the nation's capital after the war. Considering him a "safe" person, they recommended him to head the newly created Timber Valuation Section of the Bureau of Internal Revenue's Natural Resources Division. Once again, the salary of $5,000 proved to be an irresistible improvement over his current income; moreover, he could pay almost as much in order to get good men to help him. He therefore was able to "steal" several former associates from the Forest Service, including Carl M. Stevens, who had succeeded him as assistant forester in District One. But when he tried to get Girard, another onetime aide, Graves personally blocked the transfer. Indeed, the chief himself soon after resigned, protesting the low federal salary scale for foresters.

Mason and his team gathered information that was to be used to enable Congress to write new tax forms for 1920. While Stevens traveled east, Mason met with hundreds of lumbermen and their lawyers and accountants in the upper Midwest and Far West. The questions that he asked were the same ones he had used in the Inland Empire survey five years before: the extent of capital investments, indebtedness, stumpage values, and use of any forest management methods. When some of the lumbermen in turn pressed him to secure exclusion of certain types of assets from taxation, he was happy to speak on their behalf to his superiors in support of such adjustments.

In addition to the great amount of information he acquired at these meetings, Mason learned that a knowledge of accounting was the key to understanding problems involved in forest management. The postwar economic depression had deepened traditional concerns. In just two years, lumber prices had dropped nearly 40 percent. As Mason described the situation, forest owners were paying prosperity-level taxes in a shrunken market. Mason noted in his reports that few of these enterprisers had specific or recent statistics describing their businesses or employed accountants able to answer federal questionnaires. With understandable confidence, he concluded that he was more aware of the economic conditions common to most members of the lumber industry than they themselves were. Drawing upon that knowledge, he began to outline the factors involved in establishing operating plans for "sustained yield forest management."[13]

Although academics had used the term for several decades and E. T. Allen had publicized the term during the war, few lumbermen even understood the concept's premise of devising cutting and regeneration practices that would ensure permanent supply. Most regarded the process as too expensive, too impractical, or too risky to apply to their own holdings, or as irrelevant to their operations. In order to allay their doubts, Mason used the tax interviews and subsequent meetings of various industrial associations to present his personal observations of forestry methods. He drew upon notes he had been making since 1906, when he and classmate Sam Dana made a trip to New England. More recently, while in New Brunswick, he had found an operation where available watercourses limited the transport of timber and thereby curbed cutting volumes during the course of sixty prosperous years. Similar physical conditions accounted for restrained harvesting in areas of the South. Mason cited other evidence that sustained yield was economically feasible. His audiences of operators seemed interested, but the promise of sustained yield aroused far greater enthusiasm among foresters. Unfortunately, as Mason saw it, the latter tied the concept to an assumption that lumbermen would have to be compelled to practice forestry.[14]

In 1919 Assistant Chief Forester Greeley proposed that industry and government adopt a cooperative program that emphasized the lumber-

Rutgers University baseball team, 1904. Mason is second from left.

Yale forestry class of 1907 at camp on the Pinchot estate, Milford, PA (1905). Mason in center, wearing white sweater.

Mason on the Montezuma National Forest (Colorado), in 1907—his first field assignment.

David T. Mason, ca. 1911.

Salt Lake City meeting of regional forest management chiefs, U. S. Forest Service, ca. 1913. Front (l-r) F. E. Ames (Portland), O. M. Butler (Ogden); rear (l-r) T. S. Woolsey (Albuquerque), T. D. Woodbury (San Francisco), D. T. Mason (Missoula), C. M. Grainger (Denver).

Evelyn and David Mason, Christmas dinner, 1915.

men's priority: forest protection. At the same time, former Chief Pinchot reiterated his emphasis on federal regulation of private forests. At a meeting of the SAF in Washington, D.C., he predicted that continued unregulated logging practices would result in a nationwide "timber famine" within a few decades. The only way to head off disaster, he asserted, was for the federal government—that is, the Forest Service—to control cutting not only on national forests but by acquiring privately owned timberlands intermingled with or adjacent to those reserves. Convinced that Pinchot also wanted government control of cutting on private forests, lumbermen charged that such a policy would be a giant step toward socialism. Pinchot's adherents countered that the lumber industry "had been and still is tremendously inert and permeated with a spirit of indifference to any changes" in methods needed for safeguarding the public interest.

The idea of extending forestry through federal regulation also sparked a continuing debate among members of the SAF. Some advocated greater trust in and further discussions with lumbermen; others offered more concrete suggestions whereby private forest owners could take the initiative in changing logging methods. One idea was presented by Mason's former Yale classmate, Burt P. Kirkland, at that time a professor at the University of Washington's College of Forestry. In 1920 Kirkland outlined a system consisting of "economic units" based on cooperative agreements between national forest administrators and owners of adjacent forests. But Greeley, who was about to succeed Graves as head of the Forest Service, indicated that the federal agency would oppose any attempt to control production by what he felt were unconstitutional violations of a democratic system based on local self-government.[15]

A few months later, Mason defended the industry at a SAF regional meeting. Lumbermen, he declared, "have not and do not cut nor destroy forests maliciously." The specter of a timber trust or monopoly raised by Pinchot's adherents, he added, had already been "exploded and discredited." Rejecting assertions that a lumberman would "never do anything on his own initiative" except under "a big, paternal Federal club," Mason urged his colleagues to consider the means by which continuous production of forest crops could be brought about. He agreed with Greeley that the states could do much more than the federal government in ameliorating the tax and other protection problems that undermined the profitability of private forestry. But he warned that the principle of individual initiative "should not be exchanged for a bureaucracy, tending to mediocrity in its ability to produce results." Procedural standards were not to be required of the lumber industry if they were not also applied to all other industries. Timberland owners, he insisted, were "slowly awakening" to the possibilities of forestry; given "a fair opportunity" to put acreages on a "continued yield" basis, lumbermen would make the disruptive "fight" sought by critics wholly unnecessary.[16]

On the occasion of Mason's resignation from the Timber Valuation Section, the *American Lumberman* lamented that the public interest had thereby suffered the loss of his "unquestioned sincerity and eminent fairness." By contrast, however, some professional colleagues concluded that Mason had become too closely tied to the industry. As he later recalled, their response to his SAF comments made him feel that he had been "read out of the party." Instead of abandoning his trust in lumbermen, however, he lost interest in academia. In spite of the great amount of knowledge and experience he had gained in the tax section work, in spite of the job offers from the University of Minnesota and the West Coast Lumbermen's Association (WCLA), and in spite of belated publication of the Inland Empire report by the Western Pine Manufacturers Association, he was given neither a salary increase nor any other compensation when he returned to Berkeley in 1921.

But administrative myopia disturbed him less than the gap that he observed in communication between teachers of forestry and lumbermen who were potential practitioners of that method. About a month after he resumed teaching, an incident served as a kind of epiphany. After a stimulating exchange of views with three of the Weyerhaeuser brothers, he took his place at the classroom lectern. As he was speaking, he noticed one student's somewhat somnolent display of indifference and spoke to the young man with polite censure. The juxtaposition of the two experiences stayed in his mind. Faced with the contrast between working with important men on matters vital to the nation's economy, or talking to small groups of young people about matters that at times seemed to interest them only slightly, he decided that it would be "lots more fun" and much more worthwhile to go back to "dealing with grown folks." When he announced his decision to resign, some of his colleagues thought he was "crazy as hell" to leave a tenured, comfortable, and prestigious occupation in order to associate with lumbermen, whom they regarded as malicious.[17]

The decision was not uncharacteristic, however. Mason's invariably proper behavior may have seemed somewhat professorial, but he had not otherwise fit the academic stereotype. Unlike some of his colleagues and mentors, he wished to harmonize, not contend; he preferred to speak to the business at hand without digressions or opinions disguised as fact. Moreover, like the lumbermen with whom he associated, he also avoided impulsive responses and guarded private information. Although many foresters and forest operators were conservative about human progress, he was an optimist. The strength of his convictions did not, however, induce him to impose his ideas on others. He was not so much the teacher as the arbitrator who preferred to work with those who wanted to be educated. He was dismayed by people who appeared to close their minds to even the possibility of progress, thereby wasting their own capacities. Such naivete often touched his dry sense of humor in private, but he openly responded to both pessimists and paranoids by trying to help them resolve the doubts that impeded their own initiatives.

With a fundamental respect for people, Mason started into every encounter assuming that he shared more similarities with others than differences. His self-effacing behavior also enhanced his performance as liaison or agent. In modern parlance, he was an ideal "fund raiser," presenting his case in one letter, sending one billing, making a brief notation. He would follow up on these steps with a telephone call or a note, merely asking the addressee's thoughts on the matter. But in every communication, he "talked money"; that is, he put suggestions, ideas, and projections in terms of what is now represented by the ratio: cost/benefit/effectiveness. The drafts of his analyses were filled with figures, details, and examples; the finished versions underscored significances and consequences, simply and precisely. Because he reviewed every option and likelihood in these evaluations, his conclusions were sharply honed and therefore impressive in brief form.

The quality of his written and oral presentation was matched by the tenacity of his approach to people and problems. In the description of one of his later partners, he was in that respect "a bulldog." He did not bully, however; he did not make demands or contrive schemes unless supported by sound argument. Instead, he was infinitely patient and willing to wait until the passage of time put his proposals into clearer perspective for acceptance. His diary entries, recorded at the beginning of each work day, were not expressions of intimate thoughts but brief memory aides. The letters and reports he wrote incorporated the five classical questions of journalism—as could be expected of a newspaperman's son. Since the days of his efficiency studies, he had learned to absorb vast amounts of information quickly and to select the most useful details. Those who worked for him had to be similarly self-disciplined and incisive. In the words of his longtime secretary, "he expected the impossible and he got it."

If he was a "bulldog" in pursuit of his purpose, he was a gentleman in oral expression of it. He restrained his emotions, avoided criticizing others, and spoke with a deliberation that discomforted some and caused them to conclude that his was not a keen intellect. But those same traits made him "smooth" company for many others. Mason's inexhaustible gregariousness was perhaps the most important element in his success as a harmonizer. He later explained that he was "lucky enough" to have had access to offices, forums, and confidences that facilitated his work. In fact, he carefully cultivated people socially and professionally in order to advance his ideas. A list of his lifelong friends and associates would contain the names of the most prominent foresters and lumbermen in the nation's history. It would also include educators, politicians in state and national legislatures and executive posts, civic leaders, and even a few headline-makers. In some instances, these friendships began in the still-unstratified milieu of the early days, when he met people who later rose to positions of influence; in other cases, the mere fact of his presence or participation in events attracted those who shared similar experiences.

In addition to these personal qualities and professional abilities, his absolute reliability earned him the confidence of parties on every side of an issue. He was not consciously any man's "tool," and none were his. A later generation, more sensitive to notions of conflict of interest, might question the real allegiance of a "representative" of lumber magnates and lumbermen's associations who also served on high echelon committees at every level of government.. But Mason candidly informed each interest of the problems and beliefs on every side, in order to bring about reconciliations. Frequently privy to plans or information that would be financially advantageous to himself, he seldom tried to benefit from such knowledge directly. For him, the main chance was not income but accomplishment.

As both a cause and effect of his profound enjoyment of people, he found travel a constant delight. He talked with associates during innumerable trips by car, train, and later airplane, called on them at every stop along his way, and thereby transformed business into pleasure. "If you had a . . . contact with a lumberman," he later explained, ". . . you visited his mill plant . . . in some small town, and you worked with him through the morning, and he took you . . . home to dinner." He himself was a genial host. With family and friends, his proverbially dour, rural northeastern heritage gave way to "a rather merry" sense of humor. He had a keen sense for the ridiculous and a remarkable facility for recalling funny moments from the past.

Mason relished the chance to introduce family and friends to the variety of recreations and cultural events that he himself enjoyed. Outdoors, he hiked, golfed, swam, and picnicked. No matter where he was, he listened to music and watched sporting events. When work or weather kept him indoors, he exercised at health clubs or played bridge. His diaries brim with notations of plays, films, and art shows that he attended with his wife and his daughter, Georgia, or sometimes alone when away from family and friends. Those volumes also reveal an increasing interest in world affairs. During World War II, entries about military defeats and victories often took up as much space as those concerning business affairs.

Mason loved to read. His office and home were piled high with volumes, and he took books with him as he traveled or waited in countless anterooms for appointments. He preferred nonfiction—biography especially—yet appreciated the talents of novelists who wrote about the small-town life he himself had known. Out of professional interest, he examined studies in economic philosophy but read those works as an empiricist seeking confirmation of his personal experiences. The messages of these books did not plunge him into prolonged periods of contemplation. Instead, they satisfied his eclecticism and his great concern for the human condition. That concern was the touchstone of his professional accomplishments.[18]

2
Spadework

Mason had resigned his Berkeley professorship in 1921 to go into private practice as a consulting forester. He had first considered the possibility of such work while he was in the federal tax section. During the interviews he conducted with lumbermen, he realized that he was "trying to educate them" about forest management as a solution to their chronic economic problems. He did not mention that thought to any of them because, as he later explained, it might look as if he was trying to round up clients. The subject later surfaced briefly in a conversation with his deputy, Carl Stevens, while the two friends were walking in Washington's Rock Creek Park one day. When he returned to Berkeley, Mason discussed the matter at greater length with George M. Cornwall, one of the leaders of the WFCA and editor of the *Timberman*, organ of the Pacific Coast logging industry. In spite of the general postwar depression, they noted, the redwood and Douglas-fir regions of the coastal states were remarkably prosperous. Therefore operators in those areas ought to be able to absorb the cost of experimenting with management plans.

It was forestry, not fortune, that motivated him to go into business for himself. He did not expect a "golden harvest" but only a "comfortable living," as he later described his aspirations. When Cornwall suggested that $10,000 would be a fair annual income, Mason divided that total by a 200-day work-year—a period that indicated his intention of spending a good portion of time with family and friends—and decided to charge a per diem of $50. Not until twenty years later did he double that figure. In making the choice between opportunity and security, he had the support of his wife, with whom he discussed these prospects during a walk in the Berkeley Hills in the spring of 1921. A further sign of encouragement came when his first client arrived the day before he vacated his professor's office at the university.

Cornwall had told his associates about Mason's diverse experiences in evaluating timber quality and ownership. Because those subjects were far more vital to lumbermen than the ideal of forest management, the consultant would have to appeal to their practicality. Aware that some of them already employed foresters as "logging engineers," he decided to call himself a "forest engineer." That title would also conform to state requirements for licensed engineers. It was his familiarity with the labyrinthine Internal Revenue questionnaires that brought in three clients: C. R. Johnson, president of the Union Lumber Company, and the owners of the Caspar Lumber Company and Pacific Lumber Company. All three operated in the redwood forests of northern California.

In keeping with his profession's new image of the "aggressive forester," Mason interjected suggestions for "permanent forest management" into the analyses he presented to these companies. While examining the Caspar accounts, for example, he discovered that earlier cruisers had underestimated timber volumes by 400 million board feet. A portion of that bonus area, he pointed out, could readily be devoted to forestry projects without diminishing present income and would probably increase future returns. He did not find such hidden treasure for Pacific Lumber, but he explained to its officials how stands of second growth could become gold mines in the future. Union's Johnson saw the light immediately: "I think it will be better for my grandchildren," he reasoned, "to have trees growing . . . than it will be to have bonds in a safety deposit box." He also adopted Mason's suggestion for a company tree nursery.

Mason illustrated his argument while traveling with the manager of the Southern Pacific Railroad's Albion Lumber Company. From his pocket, he took a handful of coins of various denominations to represent the variety of species in any stand of timber. With them, he showed how the more valuable trees would produce greater income if selectively cut than the average income if indiscriminately harvested. The manager's first reaction was a rejoinder often used by conservative lumbermen: "Trees just don't grow that way." Eventually, however, he recognized how money and lumber were sometimes wasted in "clean-cutting" (clearcutting) the forests.[1]

The first years of consulting work in the early 1920s encouraged Mason to expand his business. At the suggestion of his old District One mentor, Albert Cooper, he talked about the possibilities of partnership with H. D. Langille, another government timber cruiser who had gone into private consulting work. When the older man began to make decisions without first talking with his would-be partner, Mason found a more congenial colleague. In 1923 he joined with Carl Stevens, his tax section deputy, to open the office of Mason and Stevens in Portland.

Lawrence Merriam, his former student at Berkeley, was hired to manage the firm's continuing activities in California. Portland was at the center of the commercial forestlands of the three coastal states. The surrounding forests held vast stands of Douglas-fir, a species in which Mason had become especially interested. Two years later his personal share of the firm's income reached the level of Cornwall's initial estimate.

In 1930 Mason brought in a second partner, Donald Bruce, his assistant on the Inland Empire report. After teaching forest engineering and mensuration at Berkeley, Bruce had directed the forest measurements office of the Forest Service. Each of the three men had his own clientele, but Mason's experience and connections attracted assignments from the larger companies. The three men customarily considered each other's calculations, theories, and observations, but each had his own specialty. Mason was the analyst of ownership patterns and stumpage values in the West, Stevens the expert in computation techniques, and Bruce the most knowledgeable about mensuration, especially in the South and New England. Each partner had a sharp eye for opportunity.[2]

Mason did not work for lumber companies as their forest manager. Instead, he designed plans for multiphased forest property management that could be adopted as part of existing operations or inserted into proposed corporate mergers. He sometimes recommended other foresters who could work exclusively with certain companies, but he personally preferred to be independent, unaffected by the rise and fall of any single lumberman's fortunes. His preference was to work with companies financially able to devote upwards of 20 percent of their holdings to long-term forestry. At first, these enterprises were willing to do no more than replant cutover lands previously deemed worthless. Mason was content with as little as that because replanting was an essential part of overall management. Moreover, he was able to point to these projects as evidence of progress in the industry.

Mason encouraged broader forestry efforts, however. As early as 1921, he discussed "permanent forest management" at a congress of loggers in California organized by Cornwall. He conducted its participants on a tour of the Union Lumber Company's reforestation project. A few months later, he described tree farming in a prospectus that he drew up for the Humboldt County Reforestation Association. That organization in turn presented the idea to the State Board of Forestry. In 1923 Mason's article on the extent of private reforestation in the West was published in a trade magazine. The several steps in that early sequence proved to be prototypical of the procedure he later employed in pursuit of ever-wider opportunities to promote the cause of sustained yield.[3]

One of the more promising potentialities that Mason discovered during these first years of consulting were the O&C lands. Those 2.5 million acres of forested domain in western Oregon had originated as the unsold portion of a federal grant to the Oregon and California Railroad Company, dating from the years after the Civil War. In 1916 Congress "revested" these lands in the jurisdiction of the Interior Department with the direction that the timber thereon should be sold to compensate for the loss of tax income incurred by the eighteen counties wherein the lands were located. Because Interior's General Land Office (GLO) had no forestry program, little timber had been sold after five years; cutting and protection regulations were minimal and in any case unenforced. As a result, no payments were made to the counties. Local officials and lumbermen who had decried revestment as "socialism" now complained about what they described as the wastefulness and ineptitude of government control.

The Department of Agriculture's Forest Service viewed the complicated O&C situation not as a failure of federal ownership but as a result of Interior's traditional policy of rapid disposition of the public domain and its resources. Using the leverage of its control over fire protection and sales on the "indemnity lands"—those O&C tracts that were most accessible—the agency hoped to bring all of the reserve under its jurisdiction. In 1918 legislation had authorized exchanges of private and public acreages in order to "block up" ownership and facilitate lumbering.

With an eye to several advantages, Weyerhaeuser's George S. Long asked Mason to evaluate portions of adjacent sections that the company owned in three of the O&C counties. The GLO informed him, however, that no action could be taken toward an exchange, because it might tie the hands of the Forest Service in the event new legislation transferred jurisdiction to that agency. That was a consummation both Long and Mason devoutly wished for. Although his client's hopes were to be frustrated for many more years, Mason viewed the O&C tangle in a larger sense. It was at once an argument against "mediocre," bureaucratic, federal forest management, and an excellent ground for future forestry projects. Mason envisioned a thriving naval stores industry in the Douglas-fir region, and he also thought of ways to enhance communities in timber-dependent counties. In time these experiments in cooperative management between private and public organizations could be extended to the timbered Indian lands under Interior's administration. Mason's firm eventually found several clients interested in each of these possibilities. For example, his father-in-law, Edgar H. Polleys, had applied for federal sales by offering a cooperative forestry program on the Klamath Indian Reservation in south-central Oregon.[4]

During these same first years of the decade, Mason participated in setting another precedent for cooperation between the private and public sectors of the lumber economy. While at Berkeley, he had met Lawrence Merriam's father, John C. Merriam, one of the founders of the Save-the-Redwoods League. Although Mason had assisted the Western Conservation Conference in publicity work, he was not a member of any preservationist organization. "Conservation"—in the sense of total withdrawal of lands and resources from use—did not coincide with his belief in renewing timber growth for perpetual supply. But he evidently saw in Merriam's organization a chance to demonstrate the interdependence of the industry and what conservationists deemed was the "public interest." As he later remarked, the redwood situation resembled the problem of interdependence between capital and labor, a subject of widespread consideration during those years.

Early in 1925, the elder Merriam invited Mason to meet with members of both sides in a state park controversy. At the league's request, he examined, evaluated, and recommended for inclusion in its proposed park the most desirable tracts of redwoods in the Bull Creek Flats area of Humboldt County. While Merriam relied on his tactics in negotiations, Mason's strictly commercial methods reassured the lumbermen as well. Because he had worked on reforestation for the Pacific Lumber Company, the owner of many of those tracts, its directors accepted his report with confidence. In the ensuing judicial controversy, Mason waited until contending parties reached a stalemate and then suggested a way out of the impasse. They in turn chose him to be chairman of a committee charged with final evaluation. (Among the other members was his onetime assistant, James Girard.) Their estimate facilitated adoption of a plan whereby state funds would match private donations to buy the lands. Mutual approval of the proposal led to creation of other preserves in the state. In subsequent years, Mason found potential park values in a client's Oregon forestlands, recommended federal aid for the enlargement of the state's park system, and evaluated timberlands to be included in several national parks.[5]

The majority of Mason's professional colleagues believed that reforestation was the most desirable form of conservation. For the owners of forest properties, it would not only provide additional profit but also contribute to the value of their plant facilities by assuring future supplies of raw material. Participation in reforestation programs would, moreover, greatly improve the industry's public image in the face of frequent attacks by conservationists. The greatest obstacle to such private reforestation efforts, foresters and lumbermen agreed, was the tax levied by states and counties on the forestlands they owned. Mason and many others argued that if the basis for those levies was transferred to the annual yield of timber from the lands, operators would be relieved of an inequitable burden, and at the same time enabled to use the capital saved in long-term management projects. Those programs would in turn enhance stumpage values and thereby bring greater revenue to both owners and governments.

Because he believed that initiatives by the states were the proper source for change, Mason assisted Californians lobbying at their legislature for a yield tax in 1923. As chairman of a special committee of the SAF's North Pacific Division, he also drafted bills for introduction into the legislatures of Oregon and Washington. Because the proposed change would in some cases necessitate amending state constitutions, there was slight chance for their adoption.[6]

When those states failed to act, Mason and his associates concluded that they would have to seek congressional initiatives. In the course of several trips to Washington, D.C., on behalf of clients seeking access to federal forestlands, Mason attended hearings on two forestry bills. One of them, sponsored by Oregon Senator Charles L. McNary, would have the government provide seeds and other forms of assistance to states adopting programs for forest protection and regeneration. Its advocates hoped that it would include a specific provision for a tax whose revenue would be assigned to fund reforestation projects on private lands. Another measure, embodying Pinchot's 1919 proposal "to abate forest devastation," was introduced by Kansas Senator Arthur Capper. It would expand Forest Service jurisdiction to include regulation of lumbering on private forests adjacent to the national forests.

The opponents of the Capper bill suspected that it was designed to prepare the way for eventual regulation of private forests. At the hearings, Pinchot reiterated his earlier charge that no lumber company could be trusted to practice reforestation on its own initiative. Soon afterward Greeley, by then chief of the Forest Service, "packed" the hearing with his own supporters. One was his onetime lieutenant, Mason, who cited examples of private forestry practiced in the West. When the committee traveled to the Pacific Coast a few months later, he guided it to some of those operations in the southern Sierra Nevada of California. Pinchot's plan was, of course, irreconcilable with his own generation's belief in a capitalistic system free of government direction. Instead of the Capper bill, Congress passed the measure that became the Clarke-McNary Act of 1924. Unfortunately for the supporters of a reforestation tax, their amendment had been eliminated in conference committee.[7]

This landmark forestry legislation came at a time of mounting concern over the economic welfare of the lumber industry. Many operators in the South were moving to the Pacific Northwest, where they found conditions better suited to rapid lumber production. Indeed, they hoped that high production would enable them to escape the morass of debt, fluctuating markets, and high stumpage and operating costs. Instead, a sequence of perverse developments pulled them further down into the mire. Increases in county taxes undermined their ability to expand or replace holdings. Lumber consumption declined precipitously. The postwar boom in housing proved to be brief, and construction relied increasingly upon concrete rather than lumber. Rising costs of transporting lumber to eastern population centers dictated that only the better grades would be shipped profitably.

Although no single solution could have encompassed all these diverse problems, members of the industry nevertheless continued to look for a panacea. Some sought relief in domestic trade expansion, but lumbermen disagreed on the desirability of raising tariffs to protect national markets. Others put their hopes on a vast advertising campaign designed to encourage increased use of wood products. The prospect of selling timber to pulp and veneer manufacturing plants appealed to lumbermen who could afford to diversify their operations. Some participants at trade association meetings and contributors to trade publications argued that revaluing timber would mean an increase in competition and higher tax assessments, which would combine to force them deeper into the economic pit they hoped to escape. High on the growing list of possible solutions to the dilemma was industry-wide consolidation. Mergers, many lumbermen hoped, would provide better leadership as well as the economic basis for comprehensive planning. They would thus stabilize an irrationally glutted market. Far down on this same list were the silvicultural and reforestation programs outlined by the advocates of forestry.

It was David Mason who linked these two concerns during the second five years of his consulting business. Working with John B. Woods, forester for the Long-Bell Lumber Company, he persuaded company directors to buy a smaller firm owning 70,000 acres of second-growth timber at ten dollars an acre. By managing the billion board feet of timber growing thereon for permanent production, the company, Mason judged, could turn a doubtful purchase into "one of the best buys they ever made." A few years later, John D. Tennant, a forester for the same company, organized cooperative cutting arrangements with the Oregon Board of Forestry. With MacDonald S. Denman of the newly consolidated Crown Willamette (later Crown Zellerbach) Paper Company, Mason also helped bring about another substantial acquisition of tax-delinquent second-growth tracts.[8]

Mason was also in frequent contact with the Weyerhaeuser Timber Company's managers. As they expanded their operations to include

Idaho forests, he pointed out that the subsidiary corporations provided opportunities for new forestry programs. The owners initially called one of these new companies Potlatch Forestry, a mark of dedication to the concept of careful timber management (even though the name eventually was changed to Potlatch Lumber Company). George F. Jewett, manager of Potlatch, had been an early leader in the WFCA's campaign for private forestry. Within a few years, Weyerhaeuser had established four experimental forestry units in the Pacific Northwest, which after 1941 would be called tree farms.[9]

Mason also analyzed forestry possibilities for lumbermen in states of the Southwest and the Southeast. In the latter region, trade associations served as clearinghouses for ideas on industry improvement, but the local pattern of small ownerships prevented effective or lasting coordination of individual efforts. As a result, many members concluded that their immediate task was modification of the antitrust regulations that prevented mergers for administrative purposes. In the West, the WCLA emerged as principal spokesman for the industry's needs and aspirations. Mason consequently devoted an increasing amount of his time to meetings with that organization's leaders, with the Forest Service's H. J. Andrews and C. J. Buck, who represented the agency's Pacific Northwest research and administrative arms, and with Lee Muck of the Bureau of Indian Affairs' office in the Pacific Northwest.

Cooperative forestry, a matter close to Mason's heart, was a subject of increasing interest within the Forest Service during these years. Before World War I, the agency had begun a reclassification program to reconcile private and public lumbering practices. By 1919 some of its sales contracts contained provisions to reduce the damage from fire and cutting. By the early 1920s, it considered adding to the tracts it then maintained in the national forests. Interoffice correspondence acknowledged an "obligation" to furnish "a sustained yield of logs" by regulating access, harvest, and protection. In Washington's Olympic National Forest, for example, the agency would "encourage sales of mature timber in so far and in such manner as the cutting will not conflict with a higher use of the land . . . and providing that the annual rate of cutting is not permitted to exceed the estimated productivity of the commercial timber growing area. . . ." In the Douglas-fir region, the agency found that "patch cutting" of selected tracts could take the place of traditional clearcutting. In 1922 the agency made its first joint forestry management contract with a private forest owner, Fruit Growers Supply Company, operating near Mount Lassen in California.

But certain predispositions within the Forest Service about questions of accessibility, price, and restocking impeded further progress in private-public cooperative forest management. As chief, Greeley would not approve of inserting such topics into public sales contracts, because they related primarily to private business policy. Personally interested in the expansion of forestry though he was, Greeley's constitutional scruples and his position as a member of two successive Republican administrations caused him to oppose any such governmental interference in the workings of what he called "free capitalism." Instead, he urged states to acquire lands for "permanent forest production" in keeping with Forest Service standards.[10]

Because the lumber industry anticipated an increasing dependence on public timber reserves, Forest Service reticence exacerbated what Mason's partner, Stevens, called a feeling of "class prejudice." After interviewing many operators across the nation, Stevens concluded that lumbermen rightly felt that federal actions were favoring every part of the economy but theirs. The industry, he advised several of them, should mount its own campaign to secure additional legislation in the fields of fire protection, tax arrangements, and reforestation. Those measures must not, however, appear to give them special advantage. Stevens also reported that lumbermen rightly suspected that conservationists, who had no understanding of the economic pressures binding the industry, were poised for a new crusade to extend federal control over private forests. He therefore argued that reforestation tax legislation could provide "a sort of federal yardstick" for lumbermen without destroying their initiatives; at the same time it would erase the blackened image conservationists were painting.[11]

Mason well knew the complexities involved in possible private-public cooperation for forest management and was familiar with the layers of sometimes "mediocre" bureaucrats—whether lumber company executives or policymakers in government. Stevens' suggested campaign, he first thought, was too big for one man. In February 1926, however, Mason assumed just such an enormous task for himself. While working on timber valuations in California, he talked with C. J. Wood, whose Caspar Lumber Company had been one of his first clients. The lumberman belonged to a "Committee of Fifteen," a group of forest owners who met in various places at irregular times to discuss common problems. Like many others, they recognized that overproduction, more than any other economic factor bearing on their enterprises, depressed lumber values. As the consumption of wood products declined, overproduction became the subject of various resolutions adopted by the group and other associations of lumbermen.

Mason did not attend the committee's meetings, but Wood later described its concern about overproduction to him and added pointedly, "You have got to find some better way to handle this situation." The consultant "did get to thinking" about that informal commission.[12] If timber production was viewed not merely as output, he reasoned, but in the accountant's sense of a ratio between costs and income, then sustained-yield forest management could be the means of regulating the supply of timber in the marketplace. Moreover, if sufficiently large amounts of forestland were devoted to such programs, they would produce timber of a quality and quantity that could be precisely calculated. Future production and prosperity could thereby be predicted. In March 1927 Mason realized that he was "engaged in a crusade" that was "more than a religion" because, as he later noted, "it was a great deal more important and took a great deal more time than religion ever did."[13]

The message he preached—sustained-yield forest management—was already so well known in professional circles that it was the topic of graduate theses in schools of forestry. Since Burt Kirkland's proposal in 1920, several foresters had undertaken theoretical studies to determine the impact of sustained-yield units on dependent communities. E. T. Allen of the WFCA directed one such study for the Grays Harbor area of Washington State, but Mason felt that his friend had not thereby secured the confidence of lumbermen. Indeed, when the WFCA sponsored a forest management conference in December 1926, participants endorsed cooperation for reforestation and tax reform but did not discuss sustained yield.

Because of his associations in both the profession and the industry, Mason intended to establish a network of support for his cause. During travels in the West and East, he later explained, "I just hunted up people to talk to." No one opposed his purpose, but few were willing to "grubstake" him in a campaign "to introduce the idea more generally in the industry." He therefore prepared a paper that he hoped would raise interest—and funds as well. In April 1927 he sent it out to more than 150 prominent lumbermen and foresters. "I believe that there is a real opportunity," he told them in a covering letter, "to apply the central idea of this paper to the early solution of the chief problem of the lumber industry."[14]

Mason chose a title for the tract that employed a metaphor well-understood at a time when Americans were beginning their "love affair" with the automobile: "Putting the Brakes on Lumber Production." As he refined his thoughts, he changed the heading to one that made a stronger promise: "Sustained Yield Will Cure Overproduction." In the paper's final form, he compared statistics on the supply of standing timber in private and public forests with those on production and consumption of wood products since the century began. Then he listed every factor contributing to or affected by the striking imbalance that resulted in overproduction. Among these were tariffs, taxes, investment in equipment, and labor costs. Each situation, he asserted, could be improved through the adoption of forest management programs on a wide scale. The transformation in fact could be effected by individuals, without mutual action, without mergers, and without government participation. All forests so developed would be *"protected, reproduced, and harvested at a sufficiently moderate annual rate* [his italics] to permit new growth to replace what is cut, thus giving a continuous, permanent regular output of forest products."

In his paper, the "forest engineer" was also a statesman of forestry. He projected a sequence of arrangements expanding in scope and impact over a period of time. At the outset, "some of the more prosperous large operators" should agree to alter their production priorities to coincide with accessible stands in the public forests. Consultations between private and public representatives would determine specific sites where cooperative management units could best be established. During that same period, an educational campaign would be mounted to reach every kind of organization—ranging from women's leagues to railroad companies—to pressure Congress to enact legislation. Among the specific measures needed were authorization for federal agencies to negotiate sustained-yield management contracts with private owners; removal of antitrust restrictions to permit lumbermen's associations to set production, price, and market priorities; and the modification of tax rates and credit limits to encourage participation in the management programs. The standards of sustained-yield forestry could eventually be used to monitor lumber imports so that only those nations using such practices themselves would be permitted to trade in lumber products with the United States.[15]

3
A Larger Landscape

Mason claimed that his program would produce results more quickly than any other economic plan then under discussion by industry or government. The relatively prosperous years of the mid-1920s provided the most propitious setting for taking the first steps. Weyerhaeuser's officials were sufficiently assured by economic developments to undertake surveys for applying sustained yield throughout their holdings. Mason hoped that the company's projects would "break the log jam" of reluctance among other owners. Most lumbermen, he observed, believed that a sawmill ought to have at least a twenty-year supply of timber to support its operations. That amount would also serve as basis for the depreciation of the mill's operating costs in that period. To suddenly abandon this belief and adopt sustained yield's considerably slower rate of cutting would be a significant change. But there was one thing Mason felt might convince private owners that the slower rate was advantageous: their recognition that traditional thinking invariably resulted in more production than the market could absorb without lowering price.

The industry representatives and professionals who responded to Mason's paper expressed appreciation for the service he had rendered to the common cause of forestry and lumbering. The data Mason compiled impressed them by confirming their own ideas or by stimulating self-examination. A few, however, still thought that lumbermen were "selfish to an unbelievable degree" and were not likely to enter into cooperative sustained-yield contracts except under the "stress of circumstances" or "compelling suggestions from financial sources" on which they depended. Others insisted that the government must act first and carry the burden of costs involved in any such management program. On the other hand, several Forest Service officials doubted that the government should tie its own hands. The contracts, they pointed out, would in effect depend on decisions made by private owners, and the public interest could not rightfully be subordinated to those decisions. Some Forest Service officials believed that the concept would work only if larger units were blocked up. This plan, however, would benefit only large forest holders. Moreover, lumbermen would object to thus committing their fortunes to arrangements that would remain static while debts and taxes might increase.

The economic implications of Mason's projections raised many questions. How would sustained-yield units be financed? Some correspondents told him that increasing selling prices or decreasing holding costs would be necessary, but which, they asked, would be more desirable? "What we really need," one wrote, "is a production control," that is, the imposition of restraints at several points along the line from logging rates to milling production. Which should come first: establishing high prices to pay for sustained-yield projects, or practicing sustained yield in order to obtain higher prices? When a management policy had brought about higher prices, would there be a rush among lumbermen to cut and sell while the market was good? Would competition for potentially lucrative cooperative contracts preclude monopoly? The question most frequently posed was the gravest one of all: how could sustained yield be applied widely enough to produce the benefits Mason contemplated without the government-imposed "socialization of forests" and regulation of the lumber industry itself?[1]

At meetings of the SAF and NLMA in 1927, Mason discussed these matters with his associates, and with the help of Thornton T. Munger, director of the Forest Service experiment station in Portland, collected more data based on the experience of his clients. By August he offered a revised version of his paper to the NLMA convention in San Francisco; the *Journal of Forestry* published his remarks in its October issue. The author quickly mailed out 400 reprints of the article to leaders of the lumber industry throughout the nation. Employing a Pinchot-like warning that the 42 billion board feet of softwood annually consumed would exhaust available supplies within thirty-seven years, he called for an industry-wide limitation of acreage cut that would equal estimated productive capacities. That equation he felt, should be applied to any forest supplying an effective plant at near capacity or supporting a community whose economy was substantially dependent on the continued prosperity of that plant. To those who winced at the idea of curtailment, he offered a plan for "birth control" of new production facilities. It was, he insisted, the only alternative to "criminal abortion"—that is, indiscriminate cutting.[2]

The immediate result of Mason's crusade was a drop in his personal income to half its previous total. His partners worried that the time and energy he devoted to his cause was also affecting the firm's business. "Haven't made much money this year," he noted happily, "but [I] think that the sustained yield idea is really started." At the onset, he had spent about $6,000 without backing from anyone but noted that it was "worth the trouble and the cost." Indeed, several men of great influence would soon come to his support by "preaching the gospel." Among the most important was William Greeley, who in 1928 would resign as Forest Service chief to become secretary-manager of WCLA. The two men were in fact so similar in their viewpoints that Mason often referred to "Greeley's and my forest policy." Greeley indicated that he would go as far as he could in bringing the matter to the attention of the Forest Service.

When Mason went to Washington, D.C., in the fall of 1927, his friend, District Six Forester Christopher M. Granger, told him of tentative plans to establish about thirty sustained-yield units in the national forests, twenty-three of them west of the Cascades. Interim cooperative contracts would be employed, Mason was told, "as soon as [the] public will stand for it." Two leaders of American forestry, Charles Lathrop Pack and Raphael Zon, also expressed enthusiasm for Mason's program. Mason's old mentor, Earle H. Clapp, urged him to apply to the more prosperous lumbermen he knew for a thousand-dollar annual retainer for the next five years. Mason also talked with Oregon's Senator Charles L. McNary. Ovid Butler thought that the SAF might well hire Mason as its own publicist. But the consultant still preferred to keep his lance free.[3]

The most encouraging incident of his stay in the nation's capital was a meeting with Herbert Hoover, secretary of commerce. The former California engineer was regarded by millions of Americans as a tribune for business at the highest levels of government. He was already widely supported for the Republican presidential nomination. Through the efforts of several friends, Mason received a letter of appointment to Hoover's secretary. Axel Oxholm, Hoover's adviser on industrial standardization, urged Mason to overcome a professed reluctance and make the call. On November 23 the consultant met with Hoover for fifteen minutes. In that short time, he introduced himself—tactfully—as a forest engineer, happily noted that Hoover was familiar with the problems of the lumber industry, and presented a succinct description of sustained yield as a way out of the dilemma of overproduction. His host replied: "That's the first scheme that I've heard of that sounds as though it would work." At Hoover's request, Mason sent him a copy of a speech on the subject he had just delivered to the United States Chamber of Commerce. When he returned to Portland, he urged associates to support Hoover's presidential candidacy in 1928. The ensuing victory at the polls, Mason wrote in his diary, was "a wonderful landslide."[4]

Along with many other professionals and businessmen, Mason expected that the coming of the "Great Engineer" to the White House would herald the dawn of a new era of scientifically planned and efficient growth for the nation's economy. To prepare for such progress, the SAF appointed a committee to conduct an "Industrial Forestry Inquiry." Its task was to learn how extensively "conscious effort" was being made to grow timber by managerial means. Both Greeley and Mason participated in the survey, along with members of the federal forest agencies. Their working definition of industrial forestry included the phrases: "the employment by individual or corporate entities in commercial woods operations of methods of silviculture and forest protection that are gauged to promote the continuous growth of forest crops. It may or may not imply sustained production." The surveyors ultimately found few instances of plans that fit their definition. Butler therefore called for a Forest Conservation Congress to consider an overall program for industrial forestry and was encouraged when Oregon pine lumbermen immediately pledged themselves to selective logging wherever possible. Most lumbermen, however, persisted in their belief that sustained yield was "no panecea nor is it possibly of practical universal application."[5]

The Forestry Committee of the Portland Chamber of Commerce—with Mason as a very active member—secured consideration of a reforestation tax bill in 1929. But the Oregon state legislature declined to pass it partly because of objections from operators who claimed that they could no longer afford to undertake reforestation, especially in a short period of time.

Mason was also disappointed in his expectations that federal agencies would be cooperative. Greeley's successor as chief of the Forest Service was Robert Y. Stuart, Mason's predecessor in District One days. Another member of that old team, Ferdinand A. Silcox, (recalled in 1933 to be chief), advised Mason that the agency believed strongly in keeping government out of business. As a result, the Forest Service would not approve Mason's plan for a joint private-federal sustained-yield unit on the Clearwater River in the Pacific Northwest. Another of his proposals, this one to put timber ownership in the Quinault and Klamath Indian reservations on a sustained-yield basis as an answer to the current debate on "Lo, the poor Indian," was probably filed away at the Interior Department.[6]

Undaunted, the consultant resumed "preaching the gospel" in the October 1929 issue of the *Timberman*. Introduced by the editors as "a forest engineer" and "a high class mathematician" respectively, he and his partner Bruce wrote that selective logging in the Douglas-fir region "can and should be based upon the application of science such as has proven so important and effective in other industries." But the policy was not merely a matter of following silvicultural procedures. Indeed, "Silviculture, if any, comes solely as a by-product. . . . On the contrary, our approach to the problem is, 'How can the most money be made from this particular property?'" In the next issue of the same journal, Mason explained that sustained yield was not based on the dubious calculations of traditional cruising but on a precise measurement of the amount to be cut each year, so that a permanent future supply could be obtained from stands of second-growth timber.[7]

The same month that the first article was printed, the nation's economy was shaken by the crash on Wall Street. By 1930 the output of the lumber industry had fallen to one-half its 1929 volume. Within two years, lumber production figures were down by 72 percent. As Mason sadly observed, sustained-yield programs were among the first operations to be suspended; lumbermen had to cut their labor force to meet property taxes, interest charges, and overhead costs. In 1931 the total work force in the industry was reduced by half (to about 200,000 men). Wages dropped to three-quarters ($15.25 a week) of what they had been four years before. Many companies went into bankruptcy, and communities dependent upon them became ghost towns. The flurry of overproduction during the prosperous years had left a stock of 5 billion board feet more than the market could absorb. To add to these man-made disasters, drought conditions raised the fire hazard throughout the forests of the West.[8]

But the Depression also transformed parochial economic viewpoints. In no industry did that change occur more quickly than in lumbering. Although existing or crisis-spawned associations still carried the designations of species or product—sugar pine, hardwood, box, paper pulp, for example—all of them faced the same kinds of problem. Even the most conservative and isolated operators had reason to work together. Just as the continuing crisis of overproduction had called attention to the possibilities of cooperative action, the national emergency under-scored the desirability of industry cooperation with government on a broad scale.

Several Weyerhaeuser executives were among the groups of lum-bermen who met in the spring of 1931 to consider a variety of plans for "orderly control" through joint action. The senior partner, Frederick K., cited high taxes, lack of self-regulation due to antitrust laws, and competition from public forest sales as the basic causes of overproduction. Mason was one of a few "outsiders" to participate in these discussions. Afterward, he gratefully noted that sustained yield was to be part of company proposals for industrial self-government. The Weyerhaeuser Timber Company would call for state legislatures setting standards for logging methods, fair measure, and marketing practices that would enable forest owners to set their own house in order immediately and improve the value of their holdings through forestry. Long-Bell Lumber Company's general manager John Tennant took the lead in mounting a publicity campaign designed to elicit public support for such programs. Greeley reminded WCLA members that it would take "a long steady pull" to get lumber prices back to "a living basis"; part of that pull, he emphasized, would be "a reasonable adjustment of log supply." Mason agreed with that priority wholeheartedly.[9]

Back home and serving on the Forestry Committee of the Portland Chamber of Commerce, Mason drafted a bill the chamber submitted to the Oregon state legislature. The measure included a cooperative sustained-yield management program. He also outlined a plan of economic cooperation for the Pacific Northwest. This regional program would be based on a code for fair production and for marketing practices that reflected industry's own priorities. The code would be administered by lumber industry trade associations. Mason expected that production would thereby be restored on a far sounder basis, and public recognition thereof would enhance use of wood products.[10] Many lumbermen seemed willing to adhere to such regional cooperative programs embodying local conditions and needs. The mechanism of Mason's proposal was, moreover, the essence of the Hoover administration's recommendations to other basic industries.

The president believed that voluntary cooperation among corporate, local, and state entities was the only proper means for coping with the economic crisis without resorting to government compulsion. He shared businessmen's particular concern for modification of antitrust limitations on combinations to regulate commercial activities. Whenever the states could not or did not reorder their response to new conditions, Hoover endorsed some arrangement of federal rules to encourage industry cooperation. As a Californian and a mining engineer, Hoover was especially mindful of the double burden carried by industries involved in natural resources development. For these, competition was not an ideal condition; it was a plague that resulted in waste of capital and raw materials. The oil and coal industries were known more widely as examples of that burden, but the lumber industry suffered as well.

Preoccupied with legislation that would deal with far more important segments of the economy, Congress gave slight attention to the plight of the lumbermen. Some piecemeal efforts, such as the removal of tarrifs on lumber imports, helped eastern consumers but actually further depressed the western industry. Economists and foresters urged the administration to take matters out of the realm of politics by designing comprehensive, long-term solutions for "orderly control." Responding to their representations, Hoover asked Secretary of Commerce Robert P. Lamont to bring together a commission to study a variety of proposals. Because there was no possibility of congressional appropriation to finance the work, the president obtained funds from private sources.

In November 1930 he established a Timber Conservation Board (TCB) to consist of twelve "outstanding men who have not been partisan advocates of any controversial forestry policy or program." One of them was John W. Blodgett, a midwestern lumberman who had been practicing sustained yield for several years. Another was John Merriam of the Save-the-Redwoods League, now head of the Carnegie Foundation. Greeley and Allen were named as spokesmen for the lumber industry. Recommendations to the TCB were to be made by an advisory committee drawn from "the best specialized talent" in industry and government. Henry Graves, who had resumed his administrative post at the Yale School of Forestry, was one. Greeley and Allen urged the board to examine "the use of publicly owned forests to promote the general practice of 'sustained yield' cutting." As a result, NLMA spokesman Franklin W. Reed, soon to be executive secretary of the Society of American Foresters and managing editor of the *Journal of Forestry*, was appointed to the advisory committee.[11]

Mason and Bruce had just finished a projection of sustained-yield management based on the Forest Service's estimates of timber depletion. In "high spirits" over the prospect of presenting that analysis to the TCB, Mason left for Washington, D.C., in February 1931. On the way, he held a "long pow-wow" with Greeley and the Weyerhaeuser brothers. The latter gave him full authority to be their spokesman, but he declined, preferring to work for advancement of his cause instead. When he arrived, he went to the Commerce Department to call on Ripley Bowman, secretary to the TCB. Bowman, who was not personally knowledgeable about forests, credited Mason with giving him a great understanding of the industry's needs.[12]

Colleagues on the advisory committee assigned Mason to chair a sustained yield subcommittee. During the next few months, he devoted his efforts to the subject that he and many other foresters thought should be the next step in cooperative management: the establishment of sustained-yield operations on large portions of the federal forests. If the Departments of Agriculture and the Interior would suspend sales from the areas under their jurisdiction, a number of specific units could be set aside for production control. In Oregon, for example, he designated nineteen such sites. These could serve as models and sources of control data for private forest owners in adjacent areas who were ready to undertake sustained-yield production and could be encouraged by federal subsidies to finance their own management projects. These subsidies could be paid back within fifteen years. Mason also suggested that World War I veterans, a group then lobbying for direct payment of their service bonuses, could be employed in reforestation work in the national forests by a central authority—most likely the Forest Service. Others were discussing that idea at the same time. When Forest Service officials insisted that their agency was the proper monitor for these various programs, Mason withdrew his recommendation.[13]

The Forest Service's own proposals for a conservation program carried much weight with the members of the TCB. Lamont carefully sought approval from the board for the inclusion of sustained yield as a topic on the agenda, and Wilson Compton of the NLMA secured the cooperation of Chief Stuart in soliciting the president to apply a "moratorium" on any new sales of federal timber pending determination of an overall policy. But neither Stuart nor his predecessors, Greeley and Graves, were enthusiastic about Mason's recommendations. They opposed sudden expansion of federal forestry and discounted the projected effects of sustained yield on overproduction. Moreover, they still doubted the desirability of attaching provisions for such management to federal timber sales contracts. Privately, Mason thought their response was "weak-kneed," but he assured his three old friends that his ideas recognized the primacy of the public interest in any contract arrangements. Among themselves, however, Forest Service officials concluded that sustained yield was "the most radical form" of production control.

Intending to revive the Capper bill's private forest regulation proposal for presentation to the TCB, Stuart was at least willing to include the idea of sustained-yield units to bolster chances for the measure's adoption. He ordered a field investigation to be made in the Pacific Northwest, a region evidently chosen on Mason's suggestion, and, on recommendation from the same source, selected Fred Morrell and Fred Ames to conduct the study. Several months later, Morrell reported that sustained yield, "an idea as old as forestry itself," could best be carried out by federal purchase and exchange of private lands. That, in Mason's opinion, was nothing less than selling back what operators already owned. Nor did the two federal foresters share his confidence that the lumbermen would readily participate in a cooperative management program. Instead, they predicted that operators would find it unprofitable, and the mergers necessary for qualifying would not easily be brought about. Repeating the concern expressed in the Forest Service's initial study a decade before, Morrell and Ames pointed out that private interests would actually be determining annual cut in such a program. Coordinated public and private forestry should therefore be applied only when the effect on production was extensive and could be shown to be in the public interest.[14]

Anticipating the negative report, Mason pressed his campaign a step further. With Bruce as coauthor, he rewrote the articles of 1927 and 1928. The result, published by his firm in October 1931, was a handsome booklet called *Sustained Yield Forest Management as a Solution to American Conservation Problems*. Designed for an audience not familiar with the technical references of the earlier tracts, the work addressed the new central question of proper government-industry relationships. A cooperative forest management policy, it asserted, would enable federal administrators to control the method of handling privately owned timber without controlling the industry itself. The TCB welcomed the argument, but Mason received letters from lumbermen and foresters who judged the idea impractical without comprehensive federal and state legislation. He did not, however, share one friend's conclusion that the "vanity and greed" of lumbermen was real or widespread.[15]

When the sustained yield subcommittee next met, Mason and Graves engaged in a heated debate over the proposal for cooperative forestry. Recognizing that his old mentor was defending the Forest Service's administrative ambitions, Mason shifted tactics. He supported the agency's call for federal acquisition of lands, ostensibly for sustained yield, and urged immediate application of such management to Interior's O&C and Indian forests. The latter recommendation brought heartening results immediately. Lee Muck of the Indian Bureau issued a report that included Mason's emphasis on sustained yield as bringing "method and order" and establishing "a state of equilibrium" in cutting marketing. Development of forest property would thereby become "a moral business enterprise." Members of the TCB evidently liked that emphasis as well and duly adopted Mason's recommendations. "Everything has worked out beautifully for sustained yield," he happily reported to his wife.[16]

When he returned to Oregon, he found another reason for optimism. Representatives of pine forest owners from the Pacific Northwest, California, and the Black Hills, representing companies holding 30 billion board feet of timber, had combined in a new organization called the Western Pine Association (WPA) with headquarters in Portland. Its guiding spirit was J. P. (Phil) Weyerhaeuser, Jr., who had moved to Tacoma, Washington, to head the production operations of the family business. Another of the WPA's organizers was Edgar Polleys, Mason's father-in-law. In view of the confidence expressed by these and other friends, it was no surprise when the consultant was nominated for the post of manager. Initially, he discounted his qualifications for administrative work but soon decided that the post "offered some very interesting opportunities." In reply to the nomination, he asked for an annual salary of $18,000 and was gratified to have it confirmed. When he accepted, the partnership had to be renamed Stevens and Bruce.

WPA's directors expected Mason to be "as nearly a czar as possible." But he was not suited by character or personality to be a dictator. Instead, he thought of his role as that of a "speed cop" for the western pine industry. Although he assumed firm authority over staff selection and personnel policy, he never rejected resolutions by members of the working committee, because they had "a lot more" knowledge than he did.

He was, however, their principal idea man. It was his paramount purpose to make the WPA a model of cooperative forestry. Because management agreements were particularly feasible in the region, he revised his chamber of commerce proposal as a "Northwest Economic Plan" that would include lumbermen, banks, and railroad companies working together in "super, intra, and inter-industry cooperation." Believing that "the bigger they were, the more willingly they cooperated," he assessed members ten cents per thousand board feet to finance the establishment of "production-marketing-price" control under WPA auspices. Relying on his own contacts with foresters, lumbermen, and local government officials, he attended trade and professional conferences to explain his plan. The possibility of a single corporation to regulate production interested many of his friends but only a few larger forest owners were willing to participate in it.[17]

Anxious to present the WPA program to the TCB, Mason returned to Washington, D.C., in April 1932. Being in the nation's capital, he noted in his diary, was like working in "a house on fire." As the economic crisis deepened, rancor marred the meetings between government and business officials. Disagreements threatened to destroy the TCB as well. Allen abandoned the cause of sustained yield and, with the Forest Service, opposed endorsement of the idea in the final report. Evidently referring to TCB Secretary Ripley Bowman's regard for him, Mason had confided to his wife that "the ways" were "greased" to put in his material. In June, however, the board merely announced that it supported congressional legislation permitting "wisely planned mergers" and "reasonable agreements" aimed at adjusting production to consumption, avoiding waste, and providing employment. It also called for tax reform. But none of its statements designated sustained yield as the specific purpose of legislation.[18]

The board's final report, Mason observed, undervalued initiatives by the industry and bolstered the arguments for government domination of forestry programs. An acquisition program by the Forest Service, it insisted, could promote more orderly, less wasteful forest ownership; any cooperative management programs should therefore be conducted under its jurisdiction. Indeed, the board agreed that all other federal forestry agencies should be reorganized as part of the Forest Service. Congressional action on that or any other part of the TCB's recommendations was highly unlikely in view of the Democratic majority's intentions during that presidential election year. Mason submitted a draft to McNary to implement the report, but the senator instead called for an investigation of the industry's plight in the Pacific Northwest.[19]

Because Hoover adhered to his belief in voluntary cooperation between government and business, Mason circularized WPA members to support the president's call for budget cuts, even though reductions would eliminate the possibility of establishing new programs such as federal sustained-yield units. As for Democratic nominee Franklin D. Roosevelt, Mason found the man's campaign nothing but "glitter and promises." Confident that Hoover's reelection would bring the beginning of recovery, Mason secured from WPA's economic committee endorsement of a comprehensive regional plan, ranging from freight rates to public relations. Using an outline prepared by Mason, Phil Weyerhaeuser explained the plan's industry-wide scope to the U.S. Chamber of Commerce meeting in San Francisco in May. Lumber associations, he emphasized, would serve as the effective machinery for "inter-economic" group cooperation.[20]

Hoover's defeat did not alter the partisan loyalties of most men connected with the lumber industry—certainly not Mason's. But they knew that President-elect Roosevelt was a "tree farmer" in private life and, as governor of New York, a promoter of management plans for state forests. The advent of his administration consequently bolstered Mason's hopes. A month before the inauguration, he noted a new mood of receptivity for experiment looking toward long-term planning and hoped Congress would empower the president ot act boldly. Sessions of the Portland Chamber of Commerce Natural Resources Planning Committee, the Oregon state legislature's economic committee, the SAF, and the Conference of Western Governors discussed a variety of coordinated plans for bolstering the lumber industry. It was with great expectations, therefore, that Mason once again departed for Washington, D.C.[21]

4
Seeding Uncertain Ground

As if reflecting the nation's adverturesome response to the promise of
the New Deal in the spring of 1933, David Mason flew from Portland to
Washington, D.C., on a new twin-engine Boeing aircraft. They climbed
to an altitude of 13,000 feet, skimmed over storms, crossed the
continent, and descended into clear weather in Washington, D.C. He
found the capital city "seething" with the machinations of men and
women anxious either to save the American system or threatening to
bring it down. Mason himself believed that a beneficial "social revolution" could be brought about through legislation. Like most Americans,
he took heart from President Roosevelt's inaugural promise of immediate, bold action. The combination of need and a new mood of
cooperation provided greater opportunities for innovation than ever
before. The new policymakers were obviously receptive to fresh ideas,
both for the emergency period and for the long term.

Few of the thousands of lobbyists who met in hotels and bureaus
were as well connected as Mason. Taking his favorite rooms at the
Cosmos Club, which was then housed just across from the White
House, he was at the center of action, if not power.

In a matter of a few days, he called at the recently organized
Reconstruction Finance Corporation to inquire about federal loans for
forestry efforts. Later he met the new secretary of agriculture, Henry A.
Wallace, over dinner and called on Harold L. Ickes, the new secretary
of the interior. Ickes urged him to renew earlier conversations with the
Bureau of Indian Affairs. Mason also talked with members of the
Oregon congressional delegation about chances for reintroducing legis-
lation to implement the TCB's recommendations.

In an effort to learn about the Roosevelt administration's specific
proposals for economic recovery, he attended hearings by the Senate
Labor Committee on a bill to restore employment in the nation's basic
industries. While others feared that the New Deal meant to bring about

socialistic revolution, he concluded that the Democrats were merely prolabor and distrustful of industrial independence. The men of "the extreme right," he noted, were engaged in a "tremendous struggle" to "emasculate" the Black-Perkins bill, a measure requiring businessmen to bear increased costs involved in shorter work hours and minimum wage regulations. More reasonably conservative men were similarly suspicious of it. Phil Weyerhaeuser viewed such "forced cooperation" as a step toward government control of many features of private enterprise. After reading Mason's report of events, he felt strongly that the industry's leaders "should choose and promote vigorously a form of Industrial Self-Government." Many other lumbermen were apprehensive that Pinchot's adherents would return to exercise a baleful influence over the federal forest agencies.[1]

Mason shared the lumber industry's hopes that alternatives to the administration's proposals would be found. While the Senate hearings continued, several hundred men representing, he estimated, 50,000 lumber companies, associations, and forestry organizations convened in the capital to consider a wide range of ideas for establishing "industrial self-government under government supervision." Hoping to advance the theories that western lumbermen had been debating since the November election, Mason called attention to the WPA's (not to be confused with the New Deal's Works Progress Administration) recently adopted comprehensive economic plan. Soon after, NLMA's Compton took a copy of that document to the office of Secretary of Labor Frances Perkins. Although the provisions for market organization and "birth control" for mills were not within the jurisdiction of her department, she liked all but one of the details in the plan. Compton, Mason, and their colleagues believed that the Loyal Legion of Loggers and Lumbermen (4-L's), a federally sponsored labor union created during the First World War period, would be "perfect machinery" for new labor-owner relations. They counted among their confidants William C. Ruegnitz, longtime head of that organization in the Pacific Northwest. But most New Dealers viewed the 4-L's as no more than a "company union." Approving of the remainder of WPA's ideas, Perkins directed her assistant to present Mason's letter explaining his plan to the House Labor Committee. The author's friends in the Forest Service took a copy of it to Hugh S. Johnson, the man slated to oversee the administration's industrial recovery machinery.[2]

While waiting for some response, Mason began to sound out the New Dealers. Along with many other hopeful lobbyists, he read *Industrial Discipline*. The work had been written by Rexford G. Tugwell, whom he had recently met and who was a member of the president's "Brain Trust." Government, Tugwell stated, must not abdicate its responsibility for national economic order and welfare by passing initiative and authority to the private sector. Many observers who worried that such a stance would mean the administration would try to bring business under government control were relieved when Roosevelt linked several corollaries of federal responsibility into a "partnership" for comprehensive economic rehabilitation. The network would consist of "Government and farming and industry and transportation . . . a partnership in planning, and a partnership to see that the plans were carried out." Such arrangements, Roosevelt assured apprehensive businessmen, did not include sharing profits between government and its citizens. Mason put aside some of his partisanship and described the new president as "the best politician we have had since T.R."

Lumbermen anticipated that Roosevelt's concept of a "partnership" coincided with their own notions of "industrial self-government." Indeed, Mason thought the term resembled his economic plan for WPA. He may have found an echo of one of his TCB recommendations in the newly passed legislation that set up a Civilian Conservation Corps to use local workers on federal forests. But other advisers were also offering bases for defining the term partnership. One proposal came from Ward Shepard, former head of the Harvard Forest and now adviser to the Interior Department. Sharing the view of many other New Dealers, he felt that lumbermen were merely "playing for time" by claiming commitment to conservation. The only way to stabilize that industry, he wrote the president, was to link production control to sustained-yield forest management. Harvest quotas would be determined by a special forest committee of the National Recovery Administration (NRA). Among those whom he recommended as members of that committee were Compton, Graves, Butler, and "an able and influential exponent" of forestry—Mason.

Although he had been talking with Shepard, Mason did not know of his letter until many years later. Had he known of it at the time, he may have seen it as a conscientious effort to give concrete form to the recommendations of the TCB. He certainly would have considered it a more desirable alternative to another proposal that reached the president two weeks later. Transmitting the views of the Forest Service, Secretary Wallace argued that numerous defaults and reductions in lumber operations made the time most propitious for permanent programs. These would not only cure the industry's chronic instability but would also establish forest management as the basis for private ownership. If through their trade associations, lumbermen were to be governed by "some definite provision" for controlling destructive logging, the Forest Service was the proper administrator of such an arrangement.[3]

Leaders of the lumber industry feared that their requests for federal assistance in the form of antitrust law modifications, tax credits, and increased appropriations might be lost in the rush to set up the national economic recovery machinery. Hoping to define "partnership" themselves, the NLMA called 100 major industry representatives to a meeting in Chicago in May 1933. The conference seemed to many a Continental Congress, prepared to reshape the industry's internal structure and its relationship with government as well. Statements made by participants and those who later recalled the sessions indicate clearly that the lumbermen were not crying for help from the federal government. Nor did lumbermen conclude that centralization was needed, even within their own ranks. In every forested region, lumber associations were meeting during those months to formulate concrete programs for production based on local conditions and local practices. Moreover, the federal recovery plan recognized that trade associations rather than government agencies were the natural and logical source for fair trade practice codes and the administrative instrument for their application. That acknowledgment encouraged the members of the Chicago meeting.[4]

There were, to be sure, some who advocated a "Constitution" for the industry rather than "Articles of Confederation." Mason was instrumental in blocking their efforts. Having returned briefly to Portland, he and WPA executive S. Van Fullaway composed a resolution that reiterated regional bases for cooperative action while pledging adherence to NRA codes for industry-wide practices. Mason then traveled to Spokane, Klamath Falls, and San Francisco to explain to other trade associations how national regulations would affect them and to help pine and redwood lumbermen work out their own codes. On his return trip to Chicago, he stopped in St. Paul to attend a three-day discussion of these matters held at the Weyerhaeuser Sales Company. As a result, he was able to accurately represent the views of important segments of the industry when he met with NLMA colleagues.

NRA administrator Hugh S. Johnson sent his deputy, Dudley Cates, to address the Chicago conference. Employing the lumbermen's own term, "industrial self-government," he affirmed the Roosevelt administration's belief in a partnership between equals. The only condition to that arrangement was a federal veto over actions contrary to the public interest. The government, he assured the assembled lumbermen, would rely on the courts to enforce code compliance. Cates' presentation did not, however, express the philosophy of many New Deal policymakers. If lumbermen were determined to preserve their traditional independence, federal administrators were equally determined to save the industry in spite of itself. (Historians continue to disagree about which side was being disingenuous during these first "Hundred Days" of the New Deal.)

The NLMA's Chicago conferees immediately set up an Emergency National Committee (ENC) to design a facility to work with NRA. Mason was named as WPA spokesman to the ENC, with full authority from the former to act in every matter. As he later pointed out, many of the provisions of the subsequent lumber code reflected the concerns he had addressed in the WPA's economic plan ten months before. Indeed, he asserted that the code itself was "modelled on" the WPA's plan. The ENC at once divided between those who wanted to centralize the administrative structure with NLMA as its executive, and those who argued for decentralizing authority to the regional level. Compton and Phil Weyerhaeuser were among those favoring centralization, and Mason and Greeley supported decentralization.

The question turned on the powers to be exercised by local trade associations over companies and operators not included in their membership. For example, Mason spent much of his time at the meetings trying to allay dissension on that issue in the Southern Pine Association (SPA) and in the California White and Sugar Pine Manufacturers Association. After one ENC session wrangled on late into the evening, he, Greeley, and a few others secured adjournment and then convened their own "rump" gathering at a nearby hotel. They suspected—evidently without foundation—that Compton wanted to become "czar" of the industry's code machinery. But they did not wish to overthrow his position in NLMA. Instead, they communicated their arguments directly to the NRA.[5]

Although many of his colleagues objected to the government's limitation of a thirty-hour work week and to the idea of "birth control" for new production, Mason supported both plans. But he stood with a majority of lumbermen in opposing NRA price control as unnecessary. Fearing that a fight on such details might delay prompt confirmation of the industry's code recommendations, the ENC quickly completed its design for an administrative entity through which the code could be applied. The Lumber Code Authority (LCA) was to be independent of NLMA but would rely on the facilities of that organization to coordinate trade associations throughout the forested areas of the country. In agreements made with NRA, the LCA would carry out the provisions of the code and oversee compliance thereto. It would thus be at once a quasi-independent and quasi-official agent of federal laws. The margins of authority in this overlapping arrangement were, unfortunately, only vaguely defined, partly because of necessary haste, but also because lumbermen assumed that all controls would end after two years.[6]

Until that arrangement could be confirmed by the Roosevelt administration, Mason concentrated his personal efforts on putting forestry practices into the lumber code. Perceiving that sustained yield did not loom large in the thoughts of most of his associates at Chicago, he did not champion the concept, but he still hoped to keep it on the agenda. He presented the matter to the ENC and then continued to talk to members as they traveled to Washington, D.C. (Chicago's heat had forced some of them to strip down to their BVD's, but the air-cooled train and a hotel swimming pool restored their frazzled spirits.) There, NLMA President Laird S. Bell of Weyerhaeuser appointed a committee including Mason, Greeley, and Compton for the industry and Chief Stuart for the government to draft an article of the code dealing with forestry practices. By its terms, those who displayed the NRA's "Blue Eagle" symbol would "undertake, in cooperation with public and other agencies, to carry out such measures, determined to be practicable, as may be necessary for the declared purpose of this Code in respect of conservation and sustained production of forest resources." Later, a conference between industry representatives and the secretary of agriculture would formulate a more definite program. The ENC would then submit its recommendations to the president for code amendments and for further action by the government.

The Mason committee's draft of what was to be called Article Ten (usually designated Article X) specified "steps necessary to secure such prompt change of systems of local taxation of forest property as will aid in preventing the wasteful exploitation of timber." But that phrase was replaced by a general reference to "measures" requiring cooperation of federal and state authorities; all such measures were thereby made contingent upon cooperation by the public agencies. Two subsequent provisions provided further encouragement for forestry practices. Article VIII's "Schedule C" emphasized production control and cited sustained-yield methods, while section "K" promised a 10 percent increase in the production total allotted to operators who devoted any part of their holdings to that method.

Compton, who later claimed that he was "the architect" of Article X, presented the committee's draft to Wallace as "an industry undertaking" and assumed that it would be acknowledged as such by the administration. When he and his associates learned of the Forest Service's claim to administer the forestry program, they were shocked and angered. F. E. Weyerhaeuser pronounced it "a very dangerous control." Mason privately criticized Stuart's effort as "a vicious one." It approached the industry as though lumbermen were "a group of people who had been conquered and were about to make a treaty . . . with the winners of the war." The industry was ready to commit itself to conservation, but it wanted the program to be determined cooperatively. Still without White House support for their own proposals, the Forest Service's officials withdrew them, perhaps to retain industry's cooperation in the immediate period.[7]

Late in July, NRA officials held six days of hearings on the lumber code at the Department of Commerce, scene of the TCB's ultimately futile deliberations. In his testimony, Mason explained how provisions for wages and hours would substantially increase lumbermen's costs. No one could promise that they would also increase prices and sales, he added. Cates "rode" him "rather hard" by demanding facts and figures—but the consultant had these well in hand. When a dissident Pacific Northwest lumberman attacked the new trade associations in his region that were to serve as administrators, Mason realized that Cates wanted those facts and figures on the record to strengthen the cause of industrial self-government.

The NRA took several days to consider the lumber code arrangements. During that period, many lumbermen demonstrated their support by forming new associations "for the purpose of immediately putting into effect the NRA Code" and to give "full and hearty support" to the New Deal's industrial recovery program. Mason used the time to compile data for establishing WPA production allotments. The only thing he wrote in his diary during this period was "busy." Other industry representatives spent the time worrying about rumors that the NRA's legal department was delaying approval of the proposal until they could secure amendments increasing federal authority over the LCA. Moreover, Mason was disturbed to learn that Cates had encountered White House objections to the vague pledge of industry cooperation with government in Article X. Wallace had advised the president that the industry's pledge guaranteed "far less explicit compliance" than it should. Roosevelt's comments were generally supportive of the Forest Service's emphases. Graves brought together his former associates in that agency with Mason and others in a luncheon meeting at the Cosmos Club. Mason thought NRA's ideas on sustained yield were "poor," but he revised the article's language to strike a balance of government and industry responsibility. Wallace found the change "far more satisfactory."[8]

When Cates returned to the White House with the code, he took Greeley along for support. (By doing so, he was certainly unaware that some New Dealers, including the president and Secretary Ickes, regarded WCLA's executive as a "tool" of the lumbermen.) Johnson had secured amendments to the original code, but he was not at all happy with the "quasi" status of LCA. Roosevelt nevertheless signed the lumber code on August 19, perhaps because he was anxious to have the first arrangement with a basic industry established just a month after NRA was created. Indeed, he was having great difficulties at that time eliciting cooperation from the coal and oil industries. Sharing the elation of ENC colleagues, Mason immediately sent a long telegram to WPA officials so that they could issue an information circular to their members. After joining in a party of celebration, he flew back to Portland carrying 750 copies of the new lumber code "for fair trade practices."[9]

The task of making WPA a model of cooperation with the LCA was, Mason wrote, like "a kaleidoscope in four dimensions." Anticipating that the code would "enormously increase" his organization's influence on the industry, he doubled its staff and budget, outlined code administrative divisions, and selected personnel for district surveillance committees. Hoping that his association would inspire compliance throughout the West, he attended public and private meetings in half a dozen cities to explain the content and purpose of the code and put divisive issues into "cold storage" for the duration of the emergency. At the same time, his personal efforts were focused on implementation of Article X. The fact that forests were more vulnerable to depletion than any other natural resource was underscored in August 1933. One of the greatest fires in history—the Tillamook Burn—spread over intermingled public and private holdings just fifty miles from Portland, Oregon, killing 11 billion board feet of timber.[10]

Against the backdrop of that disaster, leaders of the lumber industry evoked the pledge of Article X by calling for a conference on forest conservation. In October 1933 they met with representatives of the federal forest agencies in Washington, D.C. The latter, at the president's direction, had drawn up a strategy to commit the industry to end "devastation" and reconstruct the forests on which they depended. To that end, the Forest Service proposed an "aggressive" policy of acquiring private timberlands and requiring that any forest cut under the lumber code be left in condition for regrowth. The latter provision was subsequently included in amendments to "Schedule C" of the code, signed by the president in March 1934.

The editor of the *Timberman* acknowledged a minority view by noting that sustained yield "could probably be most easily attained through the purchase of privately owned timber by the government," but Compton assured his associates that the Forest Service's "Left Wing" would not put over anything "radical." Many lumbermen were nevertheless inclined to apply that adjective to the administration's conservation proposals. Like Potlatch's George F. Jewett, they admitted that the New Deal offered an opportunity to repair the forest system of the United States. But, in F. E. Weyerhaeuser's phrase, they intended to preserve their "constitutional rights which might otherwise be lost." Some, including Allen, supported Jewett's alternative proposal whereby the Forest Service and the Interstate Commerce Commission would maintain surveillance over sustained-yield units incorporated with all the advantages and responsibilities of public utilities. Mason still argued that the program should include a yield tax and "birth control" of mills, but Allen opposed those ideas.

Before the conference adjourned without agreeing on any substantial topic, Mason proposed that a "Joint Committee of Public and Private Representatives on Forest Conservation" serve as a secretariat, working in the period between subsequent meetings of the conference. Its primary task would be to assess all proposals for applying Article X, which, in his judgment, was "the most important objective" of the lumber code. When the proposal was adopted, Tennant of Long-Bell, Greeley of WCLA, Jewett of Potlatch (whom Mason recommended), and Allen of WFCA (whom Compton recommended) were named members of the Joint Committee. Although they chose Mason to be their chairman, they soon rejected on a point of order his recommendations for "birth control." Jewett offered an "American Plan" for federal forestry that called for sustained-yield units wherever possible. But Allen objected to use of the term "sustained yield" and was pleased when the LCA employed his own phrase, "sustained production," in its code announcements. Lumbermen were not ready to meet the requirements of a cooperative plan, he believed. Indeed, Weyerhaeuser approved only voluntary adherence to new logging regulations, even though the company still retained its several managed units. For most other companies, forestry was a matter for future consideration, not a practical means of coping with emergency problems.[11]

Still suspecting that the administration's intention was the "nationalization of forests," lumbermen subsequently complained that federal officials had failed to uphold their side of the pledge in Article X. Several of their spokesmen warned federal officials that the industry's willingness to work with the LCA itself would "stagnate," if federal forest agencies did not act "to establish the necessary public cooperation." If the "curious paradox" continued—one side applying the article while the other did not—the mutual pledge would be applied as a conditional clause. In that event, industry cooperation would "not be renewed within a decade or perhaps within a generation." However, the president's advisers were hardly intimidated by the industry's attitude. Tugwell remained distrustful and Wallace publicly chided lumbermen for their threat of noncompliance. The agriculture secretary again sought support for the Forest Service's authority.

Anxiously, the Joint Committee members observed to Mason that the "fires" of agreement had "gotten low" and had to be "pumped up again." Once again they turned to Mason as "the chief pumper." Hoping to satisfy both sides, Mason recommended legislation that would initiate federal action on subjects lumbermen agreed were proper areas: the national forests would be placed on a sustained-yield schedule, the Forest Service would include such practices in its timber sales contracts, and the "present destructive basis" for logging the O&C lands would be ended by transferring them to the Forest Service.

Mason also outlined a measure that would combine his plan with the Forest Service's acquisition proposal in an "omnibus bill." Compton urged the president to include reference to such a measure in his statement at a forthcoming governors' conference. But Roosevelt chose instead to reassert his interest in comprehensive forestry by sending letters to the governors as well as to Compton. Moreover, Wallace doubted whether Congress would respond to an administration request for legislation at that time. Mason believed that Silcox, who had succeeded Stuart at chief, favored the omnibus bill idea more than most of his associates in the Forest Service, but even the chief rejected a Joint Committee recommendation that CCC "graduates" be assigned to private forestlands.[12]

The dissension between lumbermen and federal officials at sessions of the forest conservation conference and the Joint Committee were symptoms of a far more significant doubt and resentment about the code. In a six-month assessment of conditions, Compton predicted that the LCA would soon break down unless it could increase sales, stem competition, apply "birth control" to new plants, and bring nonconforming wholesalers in line. As early as October 1933, the LCA's office was deluged with complaints from lumbermen and their associations. They could not suddenly or easily modify traditional practices to fit the new labor and harvest regulations.

Labor unions were initially anxious to speed the work and accept the regulations. But many lumbermen soon were complaining that union agents and NRA inspectors were either blatantly hostile to them or did not appreciate business problems. Smaller operators were unable to furnish necessary information or give advice to the agency, and, in Compton's opinion, few were qualified to calculate the cutting limitations required by production allotments. At the same time, owners of larger companies tried to dominate the program. They believed that the code was best administered by business people from a business viewpoint with the least amount of federal interference in the industry. Large operators assumed that the agency would be loathe to turn down their appeals for increased allotments because their ownerships constituted the largest part of the region's production sources. Charging that LCA's calculations were "getting rather out of hand," some demanded recognition of past experience and doubling working shifts as grounds for the increases. Finally, many lumbermen resented the agency's failure to control the "mad scramble" to buy up low-priced timber and the "rush to cash in on opportunities for price raises" that the code was supposed to facilitate. Owners of every size hopefully assumed that the regulations would be confined to the emergency period of a year or two and concluded that they would have no effect on the long-term problems of their enterprises.

Lumbermen claimed to be at a loss to understand "the whole basis of NRA and its code." Some agreed with the sentiments of an Oregon county assessor who insisted that the idea behind the codes was to be found "in Mussolini and Russia." But the specific basis for criticism was the paramount matter of corporate profits. Timothy Jerome, manager of Merrill & Ring Lumber Company's operations in western Washington, joked solemnly that it was a shame that the president "could not have enacted a law that would compel every man, woman and child in the United States to buy a few logs. Then we could afford to pay the increase [in production costs] of nearly 100% we are fearful that we will have to pay." Roosevelt's "Socialization," he complained, vested control of production in such newly formed organizations as the Pacific Northwest Loggers Association, whose rulings favored companies that owned no sawmills. That organization had given Jerome's company permission to log some 3.6 million board feet during January and February. Because the sum was merely half of the total cut during the same period of the preceding year, Jerome calculated he would "lose considerable money."[13]

The industry's expressions of hostility or indifference to its own code convinced some of Roosevelt's administrators that their initial distrust of lumbermen was well founded. At the same time, it convinced others that the government was betraying the code's basic purpose. The result was continual "shake-up" in the NRA. In the spring of 1934, Dudley Cates' adherence to his definition of "partnership" as self-government came into conflict with the centralist philosophy of his NRA superior, Hugh Johnson. Cates did not conceal his opinion that the NRA would fail, but according to his own later testimony, he was finally forced to resign by "labor bosses" (i.e., William Green of the AFL) who threatened to boycott the recovery program because antiunionists were among those participating in the codes. His resignation further darkened the cloud over LCA's dubious "quasi" powers. Moreover, the haste with which the code had been written weakened its legitimacy within the NRA. When NRA officials expressed their dissatisfaction with the agency and the code, lumbermen concluded that they had not even read the plan when they approved of it.

From the beginning, industry leaders had recognized that mutual acceptance and thus the effectiveness of the code depended to a great extent on the identity of its administrators. The Weyerhaeusers favored putting "a dictator" at its head. Compton's name was raised; indeed, by indirection he suggested himself. Describing foresters as "rather clannish" and lumbermen as ill-qualified, he urged appointment of someone trained in economics who could persuade the industry to hold the line. But some influential lumbermen still distrusted his "semi-mysterious way of going about things." Instead, he became counselor to LCA's first executive, Arthur Bruce (an East Coast lumberman; not Mason's partner but one of Mason's friends). After two Weyerhaeuser officials joined NRA's advisory staff, the company's owners were pleased that "our crowd stands very well with the Authority."

Bruce did not get along well with his NRA superiors and, in the spring of 1934, they confidentially advised the LCA chiefs that "it would be better for your industry and all of your organizations if you let [him] go." Weyerhaeuser's executives urged the appointment of Mason as successor. Other lumbermen had wanted Mason as "a sort of czar" of the redwood industry a few years before; later they thought he would be a good "dictator" for all West Coast operations. Because of his experience and stature as expert on factors involved in lumber production, he was certainly "the right man" to speak for the industry in the offices of the Roosevelt administration. Although he sometimes objected to LCA's "star chamber" procedures, he had frequently worked with it in determining production rates and organizational agreements, and his quest for implementation of Article X was generally supported as a boon to the industry's public image, however controversial its practical application. Indeed, he already had entree into both camps. He had testified to the NRA on behalf of WPA, asking for code amendments and pointing up jurisdictional problems. In matters of gathering production data, moreover, LCA had given him "carte blanche."

When he returned to Portland in late May, the executive appointment was offered to him. Claiming "great surprise," Mason wrote that the agency's chiefs had "decided to draft me for the job, and wouldn't listen to the effort I made to stay in the West." He tried to get out of it, but after a long discussion with friends and a shorter talk with his wife, he accepted. The WPA gave him indefinite leave. On June 5 LCA executives formally elected him. Lamenting Mason's loss to the industry at large, Phil Weyerhaeuser admitted that he was willing to let him go in order to maintain the lumber code.[14]

5

The Sapling Cut Down

As executive officer of the Lumber Code Authority, David Mason watched over an awesome domain. For the purpose of administering the code, officials arranged the lumber industry into a dozen divisions and subdivisions covering regions, species, and manufacturers (e.g., West Coast, South, softwood, hardwood, box, paper). Those categories encompassed some 35,000 companies employing 400,000 workers. On the basis of data gathered and analyzed by the executive officer, production rates, price levels, and employment schedules were set for each division and subdivision. Mason's declared purpose in determining these regulations was to distribute equitably as much work as possible to existing operations. This distribution satisfied those participants who were primarily concerned with stabilizing their enterprises, less so to those who were preoccupied with competition and growth. The WPA, for example, was content with its annual production allotment of about 5 billion board feet of timber, while the west coast and southern divisions were jealous of each other's quota of twice that amount[1]

LCA's jurisdictions were nevertheless limited in several ways. It could not depend entirely on public financing, as NRA did, but had to assess code participants on the basis of their production and then wait for them to respond with some portion of the assessment. The agency's 300 personnel were spread thinly over its immense administrative domain and perforce relied upon the staffs of the trade associations designated as administrators of the code in each divisions and subdivision. Some of these associations, like WPA, had adequate funds and a definite sense of purpose; others had neither advantage. The NRA, of course, had both the budget and the statutory mandate to enforce the codes, but events would soon demonstrate that its motives and effectiveness were gravely eroded by antipathies toward LCA and its members. Finally, the authority of LCA did not extend to two important areas: lumber wholesalers were not yet included in the code, and lumber retailers were governed by another NRA division.

Mason was not at the top of the administrative hierarchy; indeed, he was in the middle—he had to "sell" the code to both the industry and the government while retaining the trust of each that he was not the creature of the other. The NRA's Lumber and Timber Products Division was headed by Barton Murray. Not a lumberman himself, he relied on his deputy, Algernon C. Dixon, as liaison with LCA. Dixon had been president of the Booth Kelly Lumber Company in Eugene, Oregon, a founder of WFCA, and one of Mason's friends for years. But Murray and Dixon were too administratively impotent to be policy-makers. Both took their orders from the executive staff of the NRA. Hugh Johnson's associates were so involved with the more important codes that they could not become personally familiar with the details of LCA's concerns. (One of them once referred to Mason as "Dixon," perhaps thinking of the famous surveying team of colonial times.)[2]

NRA's paramount interest was in making LCA's actions conform with the larger economic and political purposes of the Roosevelt administration. Although it had a veto power over every aspect of the lumber code, the administration usually exercised its authority in the form of procedural delays and detailed objections first expressed by subordinates in the NRA's Legal Division and accounting offices. Mason and his colleagues learned, for example, that one of the division's staff members, Bernice Lotwin, maintained a distrustful watch over their directives. Although she eventually responded to their patient efforts to educate her, most of the lawyers, economists, and clerks at NRA remained ignorant of, or hostile toward, the lumber industry. Such attitudes did not, of course, deter them from making sometimes sweeping or surreptitious decisions affecting the industry.[3]

Acting for LCA's executive, the National Control Committee, Mason gathered information from participants in the code. He also received data and suggestions from many other sources: civic organizations, dependent communities and counties, state forestry departments, and legislators, among whom he counted many friends. But his greatest asset as an administrator was the trait his admirers called a "well rounded and sound viewpoint." Although lumbermen and officials sometimes disagreed with Mason's analyses, both groups trusted the sincerity of his efforts. When he took over the post, he realized that his earlier help with LCA's regulations had not prepared him for the complex workings of the administrative machinery nor for the diffi-culties involved in making changes. He was therefore gratified to have the help of the Control Committee's secretary-treasurer, Carl W. Bahr, a west coast lumberman who had supported sustained yield since the time of Mason's first paper on that subject. Within a short time, however, the executive officer's perception and dedication to making the lumber code effective enabled him to make his own analysis of its shortcomings.[4]

During the first six months of the code, Mason and Dixon later maintained, lumbermen rallied to comply with the regulations. Most of those who had not yet done so by mid-1934 were apparently unable to handle the financial and technical requirements involved in adapting their operations to the new rules. Only a few lumbermen tried to discredit LCA. Addressing the members of the WCLA, Greeley claimed that 85 percent of the region's lumber manufacturers were in compliance. He exorted the recalcitrants; the code was

> not an edict handed us by Congress or the President. We went to Washington and asked for it. We asked for power from the President to govern ourselves, and he gave it to us. Are we now going to destroy our own charter, or undermine it by recent violations, or pass the buck for honest, sincere enforcement to the association officers and the Timber Products Complaints Committee?

Mason tried to secure the adherence of those still uncertain about the code by urging NRA to amend the regulations and enforce them equitably and effectively.[5]

The executives of the NRA responded in a manner that puzzled and angered Mason and his colleagues. Whether or not NRA's officials had believed that "partnership" included "self-government" the previous summer, they did not accept that equation in March 1934. After the Federal Trade Commission publicly criticized LCA's price levels, NRA's Alvin Brown issued a report that Mason thought was "extremely unfair." Hugh Johnson first approved Brown's statements and then withdrew his approval. But the charges were echoed a few months later by a federal board of review under the chairmanship of the famous lawyer, Clarence Darrow. Undoubtedly encouraged by that independent judgment, Johnson then "exploded a bombshell," as Mason described it. NRA, the agency's chief announced, opposed price controls and intended to eliminate them from all codes under its authority. The decision reportedly sent "shivers down the spinal column of the lumber industry." With this in mind, Mason anticipated "the beginning of [a] long battle" to preserve industrial self-government.[6]

Instead of the administration's 20 percent initial reduction in prices, the Control Committee agreed to a 10 percent reduction as a gesture of support for the president's newly announced federal housing program.

It also submitted amendments to Article IX, the price regulations, but attached a condition calling for NRA enforcement of all parts of the code. Ensuing discussions with NRA officials, Mason reported, were violent, lengthy, and ultimately futile. Concluding that those advocating price reductions were trying to "wreck" the codes, Mason and Tennant went over the head of Division Chief Barton Murray—soon to be removed for general incompetence—to Johnson's new lieutenants, Averell Harriman and Leon Henderson. Apparently supporting his "ultimatum," they took him to see Johnson, then confined to a hospital bed. The latter admitted that the lumber industry would be "out on a limb," if the reductions were uniformly applied to all participants, and agreed to exempt lumbermen from the order. Having changed his mind about their code twice before, he would change his agreement three or four times in subsequent weeks. Mason found that lumbermen were "practically hysterical" over such erratic behavior.[7]

Mason and his colleagues were understandably anxious to secure enforcement of their code, especially its price controls. But participating lumbermen viewed those requirements as two-edged swords. "Personally," Merrill & Ring branch manager Jerome explained, "I would much rather take $1 a thousand less for logs and be able to run to capacity, than I would to sell at present prices and only be allowed to work before breakfast." One of Dixon's Oregon friends ascribed such attitudes to "greed and selfishness" and claimed that there was "considerable chiseling going on." But Dixon charitably attributed all varieties of noncompliance to operators' survival instinct. Mason absolutely refused to doubt the motives of those who were participating in the code. "I never saw any signs of overweening greed," he later asserted with characteristic compassion, "they weren't trying to get unreasonably high prices."[8]

Whether lumbermen were just trying to survive or were trying to increase their income, they were frustrated by the federal regulations. Most of their companies were not financially based on public securities; directives from outside the company offices were therefore startling and resented. "There is literally no such thing as private business, as heretofore understood, free from governmental regulation," the *Timberman*'s editor complained, "if it can be shown that the so-called private business is clothed with a public interest." As a group, lumbermen thought of themselves as "hard working, tough talking, opinionated, rugged individualists." The *Southern Lumberman* recorded a comment "based on truth" that operators were "spending more time studying the Code than they have been spending selling timber." Jerome spoke for many associates when he complained, "We cannot do anything without obtaining permission from the Code authority." Compliance was not, however, merely a matter of enforcement; many lumbermen could not understand the complex rules. (The price controls, for example, applied to about 85,000 different items.) A poll taken by the Portland-based *Crow's Pacific Coast Lumber Digest* in April 1934 indicated that over 50 percent opposed controls and all objected to what they felt was union labor's "closed shop."[9]

Moreover, production allotments seemed similarly unrealistic, unequitable, and inflexible. Whenever a company repeatedly exceeded its quota, LCA cut its limit for the next season. The agency also prohibited any operator from transferring his allotment to another. The rule would strangle operators, lumbermen assumed. If a company was sold—as many were during these economically unstable times—the enterprise thus enlarged could not increase its production to match its greater holdings; nor could the mills dependent on that timber do so. Even Weyerhaeuser objected to the allotments and to WCLA's refusal to modify them. In August 1934 the company sold 7.5 million board feet, "every foot of which was sold at Code prices," but it was willing to continue to comply only if its allotments were adjusted. In view of the fact that just eighty firms accounted for half of the total production in Washington and Oregon, the region's compliance record could be easily upset by a few defections.[10]

The connection between production controls and the other price regulations exacerbated the situation. Those for the second quarter of 1934, for example, included a thirty-hour work week and a 1.3 billion board feet limit. In Timothy Jerome's description:

> . . . we can only operate our logging camps about three weeks during the present fourth quarter of the year. Being allowed to operate so little makes the cost of our logs very expensive, and while we are recovering a larger price than a year and a half ago, the cost of the log is enough to more than make up the difference. . . . They have increased the wholesale prices tremendously and the retail prices about twice what they should be. . . . Of course, putting the price of lumber as high as they have has enabled us to get a little higher price for logs, but that cannot last. Unless the mills are able to sell their lumber they cannot buy logs and as it is now, I think every mill in the State of Washington is increasing its inventory every month. This cannot go on indefinitely. The price of shingles is much in the same boat; that is, entirely too high. In fact, so high that substitutes are being used instead of cedar shingles.[11]

By starting an upward spiral of costs and spreading production thinly, the LCA's regulations thus seemed to erode the very market they were designed to enhance. But lumbermen could not agree on methods for improving their condition. The initiative for keeping prices from runnning "hog wild," the *Timberman* asserted, had to come "solely from the buyer." Mason had worked unceasingly to bring that trade under LCA regulations, but NRA officials kept "cooking up a new definition . . . containing the same old ingredients." In the meantime, wholesalers sold green wood as dry and forced independent producers to accept prices far below code minimums. Circumstances such as these encouraged deliberate noncompliance. The Fisher Body Company of Michigan, for example, blatantly pointed up federal impotence by paying 10 to 15 percent below LCA prices for lumber used in auto construction. Citing such instances, WCLA's trustees considered withdrawing their organization as an administrative agent. Mason anxiously urged them to reconsider, arguing that they would lose their stabilizing influence over other code members. Nevertheless, declaring that 50 to 60 percent of all lumber transactions in their region were made outside the code, they voted to abandon price controls.[12]

Mason was doubtless annoyed and disappointed with lumbermen's noncompliance, though characteristically he did not strongly express those feelings. Violations were heaviest in the Southern Pine Division because many members there owned small mills, which were dependent upon local wholesalers and were less easily watched by administrative agents. (Some of these so-called "peckerwood" operators had no permanent address for revenue collectors to use.) Moreover, labor costs in that region were in such striking contrast to those in the West (12¢ and 24¢ an hour respectively) that a special cost deferential had to be applied to operations there. One Alabama operator asserted that LCA's system was really "a code of unfair competition" and "a cruel bit of nonsense" under which violations were practiced "openly and flagrantly . . . every day by mills of all sizes." Another lumberman urged that "the proper and self-respecting thing for the lumber industry to do" was to advise NRA and the president that "it will have nothing more to do with the Lumber Code [as] now written."[13]

Mason and his LCA associates rarely acknowledged the obvious fact that code enforcement partly depended on the vigilance and determination of the industrial associations charged with supervising compliance. They were outspoken, however, in demanding better understanding and support by NRA. That agency, many other observers believed, epitomized the worst characteristics of bureaucracy. Generally, lumbermen used the term "bureaucrat" to account for the inadequacies of the lumber code. Mason rarely employed the word at the time, but he and his associates later concluded that bureaucrats were responsible for a drift "more and more . . . toward what we felt [was] a kind of emasculation of self-government." NRA officials, he complained, were usually "tied up" or "out of town." After a year and a half in office, NRA staff members were overwhelmed with the volume and complexities of work involved in monitoring tens of thousands of participating companies in dozens of industrial codes. A rapid turnover of personnel further compounded inconsistencies and confusion. But even the professional people, Dixon observed, had "no business experience, . . . had never financed, operated, or had any part in business," yet "were able to tell businessmen with a lifetime of experience, thousands of employees, payrolls running into the millions, and who were tax payers of consequence, what they could and could not do under the code. . . ."[14]

From the beginning of his service as LCA executive officer, Mason made "vigorous efforts" to establish closer contact with the heads of NRA than could be established through regular channels. In June he headed a special committee to confer with NRA officials on "the emergency facing the industry's code administration." In August 1934 C. E. Adams, the new Lumber Division chief, encouraged him to expect help in getting "the treatment which we deserve" from the administration. Adams obtained a letter of intent from NRA's field administrator, and he himself conferred on the pressing matter of amending the lumber code and sent Mason to the White House to discuss procedures with presidential secretary Marvin H. McIntyre. Mason brought a memorandum he had prepared for Roosevelt, who was about to confer with Johnson. In it, he reiterated that elimination of price controls would take "the backbone" out of the code, thus affecting wages, credit, and compliance. The collapse of the lumber code would in turn undermine the credibility of the entire NRA. The president, he urged, should make a public statement denying any intention of removing the controls from the lumber code. McIntyre advised Mason that it would be more appropriate for James A. Moffett, head of the Federal Housing Authority, to make the statement because of its bearing on the administration's housing program. After waiting a long time to get an appointment with that official, the LCA executive officer explained to him that lumber purchasers were "shell-shocked" by rumors of price control elimination and "fearful to buy" wood products. Moffett expressed sympathy and promised to take it up with the president.

Because Dixon believed that the administration's policymakers recognized the connection between the stability of the lumber code and the NRA, Mason turned to him for advice and support. By August 1934 the two colleagues agreed that the interagency relationship was heading toward "a very dangerous situation." The parent body was showing "a very strong tendency to abandon the 'partnership' idea and industrial self-government." Mason warned his associates back home that "serious revolution" might occur if the New Deal failed to work effectively, and added, "we *must* make it work." The following month he submitted a memorandum that was, he admitted, "frank to the point of being offensive." He urged Dixon to consider it carefully before sending it on to his superiors. Employing the southern mill owner's phrase, "a code of *Unfair* competition," he decried the way that "honest code observers are nailed to the cross, while their business is being stolen by code violators." Hamstrung by a bureaucracy that "practically vetoes policies determined by the President," NRA was doing very little to remedy the crisis.[15]

Mason was aware that a philosophical struggle was going on within the "Brain Trust," resulting in the exodus of those who clung to the concept of "partnership," as spokesmen like Dudley Cates had initially defined it. Now the remaining advisors were assuming greater influence and, Mason believed, betraying the original concept. LCA's machinery was "far from perfect" and needed overhauling, he admitted to NRA's Leon Henderson. But "far too much of our time is occupied in largely fruitless efforts to get our partner to do his part." That partner had failed to support enforcement of the codes. Moreover, it gave "aid and comfort to a chiseling minority," viewed the efforts of the vast majority in the industry with "unjustified suspicion and antagonism," and sounded alarms that disturbed markets and stimulated code violations.

The onetime "founding father" of the code now compiled a Jeffersonian list of NRA's sins: it had permitted other code authorities to "prosecute and annoy LCA"; it had failed to establish a wholesale division; it had charged small mill owners special prices on government purchases; it had not followed up on the lumber industry's price reductions with similar reductions in materials, wages, and rates affecting the industry; it had issued blanket orders—amendments to the code in effect—without giving fair hearings or considering LCA's own proposals; and it had gone into business by establishing sawmills and storage yards in several states.

These deliberate acts, Mason insisted, were the result of NRA's "grave suspicion" of the lumber code, an attitude based upon inadequate knowledge of the facts, inability to recognize the facts, or bias against the facts. Officials' minds had been "poisoned by chiselers who have taken a great deal of time to arouse suspicion and antagonism." Apparently ready to abandon his general objection to federal regulation, Mason warned, "Our house is on fire." The NRA must order "necessary sanctions" to punish code violators. It should begin by publicly announcing that it would increase its legal staff to do so. Then it should "secure the President's denial" of rumors that he intended to eliminate price controls from the codes. In the meantime, the Roosevelt administration should appoint someone to review the crisis in inter-agency relations and make recommendations for improvement.[16]

When Dixon and other friends read the memorandum, they thought that it might ultimately become "a Republican campaign document"; as such, "it was worth $100,000." Unwilling to resort to partisan tactics, Mason met instead with NRA officials and presented only the part of his "ultimatum" that called upon them to enforce "the heart of the Code"—price controls. He was soon encouraged by several events. Two district courts upheld the controls; one, in his home state, issued an injunction restraining a lumberman from selling below the code levels. Dixon held hearings in which seven west coast wholesalers were charged with violating the rules. The defendants immediately appealed to NRA, but the agency drew up a contract that would bring them under the code. Henderson's office also secured compliance from lumber retailers, who were governed by another division.[17]

In December and January, Mason was among the "protestants" who appeared before an NRA hearing board. Answering the questions posed by NRA's officials, he reported that limitations on work hours had been effective, indeed had decreased yearly earnings. Lumber companies had included wage increases in their initial minimum price estimates. All that was needed now was a stepped-up housing construction program to increase production. He then submitted letters from LCA members, including the Hardwood Division Manufacturers Association, a group he described as "anxious to preserve the unity and industrial cohesion" brought about by the code. Another resolution came from the California Redwood Association warning that the industry's entire price structure would collapse if the regulations were not revised. In response NRA attorney Blackwell Smith assured the gathering that his assistant, Sol Rosenblatt, had "the largest dose of thyroid of anybody I have ever personally had contact with. . . ." Rosenblatt, Smith assured, would "produce results if anybody can produce them." Privately, however, Smith believed that the price levels could not be enforced or even maintained for very long. Because of the volume of complaints from small operators, minimum price provisions were subsequently ended.[18]

By way of fulfilling their own prophecy, NRA officials in fact decided in secret to eliminate minimum price provisions from all codes. The official announcement did not surprise Mason, although it did confirm that LCA was not waging a lonely battle. "Obviously our Code has just had a major operation," he informed LCA members. "Some have favored the operation and some are bitterly disappointed to see it carried out." However the fact was viewed, he believed that the industry would survive the shock. Switching to another metaphor, he urged lumbermen to "clear away, as quickly as possible, the wreckage caused by the storm" and "reorganize under new conditions, with the object of getting the very best results possible."[19]

Privately, Mason shared his father-in-law's premonition that elimination of price controls would lead to the end of production controls as well. If that happened, it would mean that the big companies would return to "the old cutthroat game." Publicly, Mason was more optimistic. The lumber industry still had "just about everything" it needed in pre-code days to "save the remainder of our Code" in some form. At a meeting of 500 code adherents in New Orleans, he announced that over 85 percent of them were supporting both price and production regulations. If the NRA officials were nevertheless disappointed with the lumber code, he asked them, "What will you do to repair the damage you have done?" When no answer was forthcoming, the Control Committee considered dismantling the code's administrative structure. Instead, Mason recommended that it hold no more meetings pending reorganization of the federal recovery administrative machinery. Every week, the mail brought him resolutions from administrating associations that considered or resolved to withdraw from the code. NRA officials were quick in their response to that, at least. If any agencies of the lumber code withdrew from their responsibilities, they warned darkly, NRA and not LCA would choose their replacements.[20]

Addressing Yale School of Forestry students in January 1935, Mason made no mention of the administrative impasse. The following month, however, the matter was made public at NRA hearings. After a southern lumberman testified that LCA's ruling could not be enforced even if the government put "whole communities in the hoose-gow," Leon Henderson angrily objected to LCA's complaints about enforcement. Fourteen percent of NRA's legal actions, he insisted, were pressed on behalf of the lumber code. LCA, he countercharged, was contributing to price fixing by ordering competitive operators to shut down.[21]

Although Mason kept his hopes pinned to some kind of reorganization in the administrative arrangement with government, both LCA and NRA collided with a force more powerful than the industry or the administration. Many Americans were already anticipating that the Supreme Court would require a legislative overhaul of the New Deal's recovery program. Mason and his associates especially took heart when the justices agreed to consider the case of William E. Belcher, an Alabama lumber company owner who had paid his employees 10 cents an hour for a fifty-hour work week—a double violation of the lumber code and the regulations of the NRA. When the Control Committee tried to discipline Belcher, he secured support from a federal district judge who decided that the code was unconstitutional.[22]

Recognizing the potential significance of the case, the Department of

Justice appealed directly to the Supreme Court. NRA's Blackwell Smith urged officials to rush the matter "to the utmost of our ability" so that a ruling could be rendered before Congress adjourned. The legislators would then have time to correct NRA's statutory authority in light of the final judgment, and there would be slight interruption in the recovery program. Donald Richberg, head of NRA's executive council, advised the president that the court's judgment would remove widespread accusations that the administration was involved in illegal policies and would overcome congressional reluctance to pass remedial measures.

Other advisors argued against pressing the *Belcher* case because of its implications. These were the officials who had objected to the lumber industry's original code and had thereafter protested its approval. Richberg later reversed himself and concluded that LCA had "most unusual powers" which were "practically free" from federal control. The code that it administered "went much farther" in regulating production and prices than those for the so-called Big Six basic industries over which the government had waged "epic" fights.

The LCA—the most dubious of the codes—was "a very poor foundation for a test case," in Richberg's *ex post facto* reasoning. The lower court had not taken evidence or made any decision on the necessity for the code or the reasonableness of its requirements. The high court might only take "judical notice" of the economic conditions that gave rise to the codes under NRA. As it had in a recent decision, it might also remand the suit back to the district court with orders to take evidence on that subject. Thus the constitutionality question would remain unsettled. "This would be a partial, but rather hollow, victory," Richberg observed. Even if these possibilities did not occur, he reasoned, the government would be resting the legality of NRA's program "on the example of a code which we ourselves regarded as an unwise and possibly illegal excercise of delegated power." His inference was obvious: if the Supreme Court upheld the agency in the *Belcher* case, it would thereby confirm the status of the lumber code.[23]

Both Solicitor General Stanley Reed and unofficial but very influential presidential adviser federal Judge Felix Frankfurter argued that it would be "suicide" to risk failure just to get an early ruling on NRA. Although critics jeered that the administration was afraid to go to court with its programs, the Supreme Court had recently upheld the New Deal's grant of executive power, and the president had asked Congress for a statutory extension of NRA's life. Deciding in mid-February that a political tactic was as important as a legal point, Roosevelt directed the Justice Department to withdraw its appeal in the *Belcher* case.[24]

Mason did not learn of the decision until March 22, when Smith and

Stanleigh Arnold of the Justice Department took him to lunch and dropped this last straw on the lumber code's back. Although they did not reveal the source of the final decision, Mason privately concluded that it was Roosevelt himself. Lumbermen who had written their code and created the LCA were, in Mason's opinion, "justifiably outraged." After months of extensive cooperation with the federal program that constituted "a marked contribution" to industrial recovery, they had been "thrown to the wolves" in order to improve NRA's chance for survival. The government had thereby greatly diminished the likelihood that the industry would confidently participate in any reorganization of the program, whether by legislation or executive action. Lumbermen still felt that the administration needed the lumber code more than the industry needed NRA. If the code was not dissolved, it would be "emasculated" and, in that condition, imposed even while enforcement continued to be ineffective.[25]

Mason at once discharged most of LCA's staff members—"including myself," he noted—and called on LCA members to decide on their own future. Of the organizations, companies, and individuals participating in the lumber code, 22,637 voted to suspend the arrangement and 8,515 voted to keep it. Among the latter, Mason proudly observed, was the WPA, which hoped that the industry would "work out its own salvation under the code." Others specifically exempted wages, hours, and conservation practices from the suspension, or fearfully noted that an already stagnating market would be disturbed further.[26] Perhaps it was that apprehension that promoted Mason to continue his struggle to save the code structure.

With the support of the Control Committee, he urged Richberg to reconsider dismissal of the *Belcher* appeal. The NRA executive replied with "a very apologetic" statement, acknowledging that the lumber industry had been treated shabbily. It was wrong, he recognized, for the government to assume that because lumbermen had made "no front page battle" over the code in 1933 and had avoided controversy immediately thereafter, that they would now supinely accept perfidious actions. If NRA was not careful, he acknowledged, it would have on its hands a "belligerent" industry whose response would make the "epic" fight for a soft coal code seem "hardly more than a circumstance."

When Richberg's colleague, Averell Harriman, met with the LCA officials, he refused to make the conciliatory gesture of suspending the code in order to secure the industry's acceptance of a reorganized NRA. He agreed, however, to speak with Mason on amendments that would be included in the new arrangement. Rosenblatt also assured LCA of NRA's "extremely ambitious plans" for enforcing compliance. (One he specified—stamping the Blue Eagle symbol on lumber of cooperating companies—was obviously rather feeble.)[27]

The lumber code was "folding up," the New York *Times* announced ominously. That claim, Mason sadly noted, was "rather inflamatory, truculent, but fairly penetrating and mostly correct." LCA's Control Committee considered making a final request to press the *Belcher* appeal. Mason drafted their petition to the Supreme Court and, when the committee deadlocked on the question of actually filing it, he broke the impasse with his vote. On April 1 the court rejected their request. A few days later, Harriman and Stanleigh Arnold of the Justice Department informed Mason and his colleagues that the government had another test case, this one involving the Schechter Poultry Company's challenge to NRA marketing codes within New York State. LCA officials thought that it was a far weaker opportunity than the *Belcher* suit. Even Richberg agreed that it was not the best choice with which to obtain a sweeping victory, because it dealt with intrastate transactions. But because the lower court decision being appealed was stronger in *Schechter*, he thought it better than the lumbermen's case.[28]

Although Harriman agreed to a plan for agency reorganization, Mason felt like he himself was bailing water from a sinking ship. The government had weakened both LCA and NRA, he believed, by abandoning the *Belcher* appeal. Administration spokesmen indicated that they would use compulsion to enforce the code if voluntary compliance was not forthcoming. Then they would issue contracts only to cooperators. But these contradictory statements seemed nothing but "a new bluff." As LCA's attorney put it, whether New Deal policymakers objected to the provisions giving discretionary power to a nongovernmental agency or whether it doubted the validity of the code, the central issue was enforcement. Even if it boycotted companies that refused to comply with the regulations, withdrawal of support by such large organizations as the Southern Pine Association made such penalties meaningless on a region-wide basis. The Control Committee indignantly rejected NRA's request to join in a boycott, calling it a conspiracy "to deprive the citizens of their constitutional rights," and would subject them to "the will or caprice of federal officers." It would be better for the federal authority to suspend the code wherever noncompliance existed "in a substantial degree" and could not be effectively disciplined.[29]

But how could the damaged ship be otherwise repaired? In their continual emergency conferences with NRA officials, Mason and his associates differed on the best design for industrial self-government if NRA was to be extended. He and Tennant favored retaining LCA and its administrative machinery intact. But there should be "radical reorganization" of its relationship with NRA. Mason suggested the creation of a "Lumber and Timber Products Board," responsible only to NRA, and an "Advisory Council" to act as a winnowing machine, separating essential matters from impractical features. Representatives of industry and government would thus work "in very close harmony," and frictions and misunderstandings could be avoided.

But Wilson Compton, in his capacity as counselor, did not think that lumber and timber industries had "even yet learned teamwork." They should therefore agree upon a simpler voluntary code—one that would not turn their interests into national issues as production and price controls had done. Urging his associates not to forget 1932, he thought they could properly expect the New Dealers to seek legislative confirmation of a philosophy whereby all members of an industry would be bound to comply with codes whether or not they wore the Blue Eagle themselves.

LCA's executives voted to reaffirm LCA's charter as the proper agency for carrying out the lumber code. They had every intention of bolstering the administrative framework and urged NRA to propose amendments to the code and promise to enforce them. Just because their members had supported suspension, they warned, the government was not to assume that the industry was willing "to relinquish the discretionary power which the Code now gives it." The LCA executives asked only that the NRA solicit their views on such changes in procedure and authority as new legislation and remodeling might entail. Mason promised that LCA would revise the code on the basis of amendments thus agreed upon and urged the NRA to defend that arrangement in public statements.[30]

Richberg promised to submit amendments to the industry through LCA; these would become effective only within the divisions and subdivisions that approved of them. Moreover, he indicated that enforcement would not be undertaken "during continuance of conditions making it inequitable." Heartened by this new chance to extend industrial cooperation, Mason spent nearly all of his time "six fathoms deep" preparing for testimony before the Senate Finance Committee, which was then investigating NRA. Before the committee, he emphasized the fact that the industry had taken the promise of "partnership" on face value; it needed supervision but had no intention of becoming wholly subject to the NRA. In the hour he was "on," he did not get as much heckling as he expected. When he learned that the legislators were determined to end price controls and intrastate jurisdictions, however, he concluded that they meant to ruin the "partnership." Subsequently, he "objected in some detail" to proposed amendments to a reorganization that involved federal control of the industry.

During those spring months, both supporters and opponents of the NRA swung wildly from hope to despair and back again. Two of Mason's clients, Weyerhaeuser and Long-Bell, wrangled over the collective bargaining section (7-A) of the NRA program. Mason's friends in the United States Chamber of Commerce roundly condemned the New Deal. Then the Senate Finance Committee voted to extend the controversial recovery agency for a year. In his spare time, Mason sat in on Richberg's presentation of arguments in the *Schechter* case at the Supreme Court and concluded that the justices' questions indicated no chance for a government victory. In mid-May he returned to Portland for a strategy council with LCA leaders on the future of industrial self-government.

There he found lumbering operations down between 70 and 90 percent because of a widespread strike. Organized labor, he believed, was "taking unfair, extreme, and outrageous advantage" of the favorable status that the NRA apparently accorded it. Because of NRA's "greatest crime," as Mason later called it, west coast lumbermen had become "bitterly opposed" to the administration's recovery program. Even if the Supreme Court or Congress extended it, the Blue Eagle on their products "would amount to a union label." In a report to LCA's divisions, Mason was highly critical of those he called union "gangsters." At first bewildered by the strikes, he felt that the industry resented such a response to its efforts to cooperate with the NRA's program. That program ended suddenly, however, with a decision in the *Schechter* case: the NRA was judged an unconstitutional transfer of legislative power to the executive branch of the federal government.[31]

Concluding that the New Deal itself had been destroyed by the judgment, Mason returned to Washington, D.C. When LCA's Control Committee met on June 10, it unanimously voted to dissolve the industry's experiment in industrial self-government. Back at his desk, Mason reduced LCA's office staff to six persons, assigned Carl Bahr to liquidate funds and equipment, and gleaned record files and turned them over to Compton's NLMA. In a final effort to communicate with NRA, he urged its officials to consult with former LCA executives in writing a history of the lumber code. Like most of his other efforts in that relationship, this request was for the most part ignored; Dixon was the only lumberman-official whose judgment was incorporated in the document. Finally, he and his wife attended several farewell parties given by surviving bureaucrats for LCA and NRA members. Mason presented his recommendations for sustaining industrial self-government to the NLMA's regional associations, assembled in Chicago, and was gratified when most were accepted pending the adoption of means for financing the program. Then he and Evelyn boarded a ship for "one grand loaf" of a voyage through the Panama Canal to Portland.[32]

6
A New Shoot Blossoms

Mason did not forget the many other countervailing forces at work in the lumber industry, but he agreed with his associates that their bold experiment in self-government had been brought down by the perfidy of the New Deal bureaucrats. "Who can now rescue us?" he asked himself. Not the politicians, for they were demagogues in his opinion. He welcomed a journalistic poll predicting a rejection of the New Deal by voters as the "best news in a long time." Instead of relying on political solutions, he hoped that the lumber industry could agree on its own system of regulation. Moreover, he believed that the industry was much better able to do a good job of forestry than the Forest Service could hope to do. A "Timber Sales Agency," he suggested, might coordinate production and marketing much as LCA had done. But he found little interest in that proposal.

As some observers had anticipated after the *Schechter* decision, the industry was just then experiencing an improvement in its shaky economic condition. Larger companies were understandably content to operate their own sales agencies and support the industry's tree farm movement. One Weyerhaeuser executive spoke for lumber companies of every size when he predicted that any combination of operators for such a purpose would eventually come under federal control. Indeed, the Roosevelt administration was already enlarging the labor provisions of the defunct NRA. Its new Wagner Labor Relations Act was, Greeley protested, "directly contrary" to collective bargaining because it placed employees "under complete domination" by professional organizers who would revolutionize the labor market and "destroy" the right to work. The "heavy hand of centralism" that they decried had even soured their initial regard for the popular Civilian Conservation Corps, Mason and others in his profession admitted. His colleagues in the SAF were therefore divided over the issue of endorsing any program of the New Deal.[1]

The enforcement of Article X by members of lumber trade associations consequently loomed as a far more desirable alternative. To that end, Mason continued to work with federal officials in order to salvage the conservation provisions of the lumber code. During his first six months as executive officer, support for those measures had been decidedly mixed. Some lumbermen were attracted by Article VII's promise that 10 percent would be added to their production allotment if they devoted a portion of their holdings to sustained-yield projects. Laird Bell wondered whether Article X might eventually "furnish a reason for consolidation of western Oregon areas into one sustained-yield unit." Those anxious to make self-government work considered these provisions as means whereby they could adjust their harvest methods to a depressed market. A few even declared their adherence to forest management in order to refute conservationists' allegations that the industry's pledge to Article X was not sincere.

Whatever the reason for compliance, Mason reported that nearly a thousand companies were developing sustained-yield programs by April 1935. Over a million and a half acres were devoted to management and, in several districts, the programs accounted for the bulk of lumber production. Ninety-eight percent of WPA's membership, he was gratified to note, were cooperating in these efforts. Several divisions and associations employed foresters and forest management technicians as advisers, planners, and field workers. In March 1934, for example, WCLA's manager, Warren Tilton, ordered members to adopt forestry procedures. Soon after, in the Western Pine Division, a Forest Protective Committee was established in each of seven units to oversee application of Schedule C's rules on cutting and restocking and to encourage adoption of sustained-yield programs as the industry's "most important ultimate objective" in complying with the lumber code. Although forestry had been "subordinated to other [code] provisions," Mason insisted that "progress has been made and we do not need to apologize."[2]

LCA's critics at NRA and the Forest Service were quick to point out that those adhering to forestry principles were but a small fraction of the operators participating in the code, but Mason blamed the NRA for that fact. NRA, he countered, had refused to approve LCA's budget requests or enlarge its administrative machinery for conservation. By failing to enforce the other articles of the code, NRA had cast doubts on Schedule C and Article X. Moreover, the Forest Service's response to LCA's recommendation to put "teeth" in X was no more than a directive to operators to leave two seed trees for every acre of forest cut. NRA refused to consider X any differently than other code provisions and objected to the agency's designs for a special supervisory program.

Pursuing other means, Mason revised the Omnibus Bill, which had been debated in the Joint Committee of Public and Private Representatives on Forest Conservation and set aside the previous year. The new measure would put all federal forests on a sustained-yield basis, designate and define units in which private and public operations could cooperate "whenever profitable," authorize sales to those cooperators, extend low-interest federal credits to them through the RFC or deferred tax arrangements, and encourage the states to do the same. Not until November 1934 did his colleagues in the Joint Committee approve of a bill that would include all of these provisions.

Like those of the NRA, the Forest Service officials tried to undercut LCA's authority. Claiming that the majority of lumbermen under the code had failed to uphold the Article X pledge, federal foresters indicated that they would support the bill only if their agency was named as its sole administrator. They saw the issue as one of private interest versus social stability and expressed special concern for communities dependent on lumber production. Chief Silcox argued that he could not let national forest timber go "to aid a form of organization which is inherently against the public interest."[3] Among the instances cited was that of Bend, Oregon, a town dominated by the operations of the Shevlin-Hixon Company and Brooks Scanlon Lumber Company. Mason had planned a sustained-yield program for the former enterprise—as the Forest Service men well knew—but the concept had not been applied even when the company was a participant in LCA's code. If the government required forestry in contracts authorized by the Omnibus Bill, they claimed, such indifference would be overcome, and companies would be forced to reorganize along forestry lines.

In January 1935 President Roosevelt pointed out to governors from forested states that improved management of timber resources need not depend solely on federal-state legislation. A few days later, however, the Forest Service resumed its campaign. Assistant Agriculture Secretary Tugwell asked Roosevelt to allow NRA to designate the Forest Service as the enforcer of Article X, and Silcox told a meeting of the SAF that public control of the logging and lumber industry was the only way to maintain the lumber code's forestry provisions. The statement shocked the industry; Mason wrote that it had "poisoned the public mind." In the course of a two-and-a-half-hour talk between the two old friends, Silcox insisted that his words had been misunderstood. He wanted the industry—with Forest Service help—to "impress upon the recalcitrant the need for compliance." Mason advised him to tone down his remarks for an address to the LCA in March. Before the LCA, Silcox maintained that public control would be necessary *if* the industry did not voluntarily adopt conservation practices. Partisans of the industry were hardly mollified. The Forest Service, Carl Stevens maintained, was trying to restore the "broad-arrowism" of colonial times (the royal reservation of the best timber). The idea was "worse than Prohibition." Even the otherwise compliant WPA resolved that Congress should forestall any attempt to enlarge federal control over the industry.[4]

Article X's supporters were themselves uncertain whether or not federal legislation to enforce the provision was desirable or, more basically, whether Congress had proper jurisdiction over the industry in the matter. Mason hoped that the president would at least declare that the purpose of a national forestry program was to establish sustained yield wherever practical, especially in the Pacific Northwest, on the basis of cooperation with state, local, and private organizations. But when Florida's Senator Duncan U. Fletcher introduced the Omnibus Bill that spring, Roosevelt offered only that the subject was "near to my heart," and promised that it would receive his support at "the most favorable opportunity." When Mason and several NLMA officials later tried to see the president, the White House secretary told them to submit letters instead. The bill's supporters therefore tried the tactic of retrieving just the credits item and attaching it as a rider to an Agriculture Department appropriations bill. Their effort failed. When an NRA lawyer drafted a substitute measure, WFCA's George F. Jewett denounced it as "a first step in a definite movement to force government control on the forest industries." Noting that the proposal would authorize federal inspection not only of company operations but of their accounts as well, some called it "fascist."[5]

Adamant against giving a free hand to the NRA, most lumbermen opposed the forestry bill. If they could not have tax reform or a measure clearly in keeping with the mutual basis of Article X, then they chose to remain "free to resist any regulations imposed" on them. Jewett even proposed that the federal government reward operators who practiced forestry by exempting them from any controls. With an administration such as the New Deal in office, Jewett's colleague, E. T. Allen, concluded, "I think the industry should do just as much as it can afford to do, and expect damn little help" from government. Even though some lumbermen and foresters worked for state legislation, others felt that federal agencies would eventually dominate state programs as well. During discussions of their own conference on the subject to be held later in 1936, many agreed that private forestry was adequate and, as Allen put it, it was time to de-emphasize sustained yield and "get back to first principles, namely, forest protection."[6]

Mason recognized that there would be a lull before lumbermen were in sufficient financial shape to do much with cooperative forestry programs. But he saw the hiatus as an opportunity to facilitate economic recovery, which would in turn provide the basis for better forestry. Returning to Portland in mid-1935, he went back to work as WPA manager. Because he found that the "strongest" of his colleagues (whom he characteristically declined to name) had left that organization, he soon resigned and resumed his independent status as a consultant. His purpose, he declared, was to make a living "by furthering as much as possible the objectives of Article X."

For several months in 1936, he had no partners; Stevens had died and Bruce did not rejoin the old firm until October. None of the consultants had done very well during the preceding years. Mason's own income had increased to over $15,000 during the LCA period, but it subsequently declined to a third of this previous amount. Since few of his former clients had the means to follow up on full-scale management plans, he had to build up a new clientele among those lumbermen who were beginning to flourish. Several friends, however, were sufficiently impressed with the impact of Article X to help finance this extension of his old crusade. Weyerhaeuser for example gave him $100 a week for the year beginning in March 1936, and Long-Bell contributed $50.[7]

In the company of such old adherents as William Greeley and Phil Weyerhaeuser, Mason became a member of advisory committees with the Portland Chamber of Commerce and the state Board of Forestry. The most important position he held was with the Pacific Northwest Regional Planning Commission. Established to coordinate surveys and master plans for the region's four states with those of the federal government, the commission acted as liaison between planners representing the private and public sectors of the economy. At the urging of its director, Oregon newspaper editor Marshall Dana, Mason accepted the chairmanship of the commission's Forest Conservation Committee in order to ensure that they did not "go off on a tangent with some new plan more or less in conflict" with Article X. In its subsequent report, titled "Forest Resources," his committee offered a detailed program for cooperative agreements supported by lumbermen and backed by state legislation. As he had done with his call for action a decade before, Mason sent copies of the report to those whom he deemed "quite important people in the forest industries."

To learn what changes had or had not occurred in the thinking of administration officials since his departure from Washington, D.C., Mason also traveled back to the capital in October 1935 and January 1936. The Forest Service, he observed, was still asking the industry to declare that forestry was its primary purpose. When Mason told Silcox what the WPA had been doing to continue Article X, the chief was impressed and pledged that he would again approach the president on the matter of the Omnibus Bill, or sustained yield bill, as Mason intended it would be called. At meetings of the National Forest Reservation Commission, an advisory body created by the Weeks Law of 1911 and assigned the task of locating forestlands for public purchase, Mason ruffled the feelings of Interior Secretary Ickes by inferentially criticizing the administration's inclination to compete with forest owners. Government should instead subsidize private operations in lower quality, less accessible public timber. He made the same suggestion when he returned to the regional commission meeting in Spokane, Washington. In both instances, he cited sustained-yield management of the O&C lands as the most practical first step for a cooperative program.[8]

Of that domain's estimated 40 billion board feet of timber—mostly Douglas-fir—only about 20 percent was ready for harvest in the immediate period. Mason believed, however, that even that amount could depress the Oregon lumber market if it was indiscriminately cut. He therefore urged that a policy of "extreme conservation" be applied to lay a sound foundation for future response to variable conditions. Moreover, the economic and social stability of some seventy companies and half that number of milling communities would thereby be stabilized. Because of the limited scope of the plan, local lumbermen welcomed his arguments with far greater enthusiasm than they had given to Fletcher's Omnibus Bill or the Forest Service's claim to the lands.

Mason, Greeley, and Forest Service official C. J. Buck brought the subject to the attention of the Portland Chamber of Commerce and the Oregon State Planning Board early in 1936. At their suggestion, the two organizations began a campaign to secure local and congressional support for O&C legislation. The idea appealed to Senator McNary, who had been trying to do something about the O&C dilemma for over a decade. The measure he had just introduced, cosponsored by Mississippi Congressman Wall Doxey, would authorize sustained-yield units in the national forests but did not designate the Forest Service's acquisition program as the basis for such projects. Dallas, Oregon, lumberman George Gerlinger, leader of the Willamette Valley Lumbermen's Association, pledged his support but warned of a "row and indefinite delay" if the government failed to consult with industry members. The problem of county revenues, moreover, still constituted an obstacle to possible inclusion of the O&C lands in the bill. Mason and John B. Woods, his fellow warrior from Article X days, prepared their lobby campaign with the hopes of bypassing both the jurisdictional and the tax issues by urging the Interior Department to write a specific measure.[9]

Secretary Ickes found his own reasons for supporting that idea. He had first noted the problems of the O&C domain in June 1933, when he suspended public sales thereon as part of the administration's attempt to cope with the lumber market crisis. The recommendations of the Joint Committee of Public and Private Representatives on Forest Conservation, made in October 1934 and January 1935, provided the secretary's advisers with a framework. They of course shared their chief's concerns in any arrangement. Sustained-yield contracts for O&C timber, they concluded, would have to be completely controlled by the government. Ickes was not only determined to strengthen the public interest, however; his paramount purpose was to renovate Interior's image and turn the department into the principal conservation agency in the nation. As part of that transformation, he proposed to bring the Forest Service into Interior. A new management program for the O&C lands would be the first skirmish in that campaign.

Soon after Ickes began considering the matter, AFA Executive Secretary Ovid Butler forced his hand. In an article in the April 1936 issue of the AFA's journal, *American Forests*, Butler decried Interior's past management of O&C timber. Even under the new self-proclaimed conservationist secretary, he claimed, federal policy was scandalous. The implication was clear: only the Forest Service was sufficiently enlightened and competent to administer O&C lands with proper forestry methods. Ickes hotly denied the charges, but he was evidently wary of a possible investigation by McNary's committee. He therefore assigned Rufus Poole, an assistant to Interior's solicitor, to draft a bill to establish a new O&C administration.

Poole consulted with Ward Shepard of the Interior's Indian forest service and with Guy Cordon, attorney for the Association of O&C Counties. Cordon evidently convinced Poole that the bill would have to contain a new formula to solve the problem of tax revenues. It was Shepard who designed the forestry provision of the draft, including specific reference to a total annual cut limit in keeping with Mason's earlier recommendation. Poole omitted that detail, however, because he knew that the secretary wanted "a simple forest management bill," that is, only a framework of authority to be filled in by executive directives. Poole's second mistake was his failure to consult with the National Forest Reservation Commission or the Oregonians supporting the Portland Chamber of Commerce's campaign. In June Ickes sent the bill to the House Public Lands Committee, chaired by Louisiana's Rene L. De Rouen—a ploy, perhaps, to minimize Republican Senator McNary's influence. It was only one page long. The secretary of the interior was summarily authorized to "perform any and all acts" that were "in his discretion" necessary and proper, including the making of "cooperative agreements" with federal, state, and private owners concerning "time, rate, method of cutting and sustained yield."[10]

There was no chance that the De Rouen bill could be acted upon before Congress adjourned that summer, but the prospect sparked a loud debate in Oregon. Among the many lumbermen to criticize the measure was George Gerlinger, who had served with Mason on several civic and state forestry advisory committees. In order to head off further consideration of the bill, Gerlinger threatened to organize a public protest. With his usual restraint, Mason decided that although the Interior Department's effort was "a step in the right direction" it still needed "considerable strengthening." When their colleagues pledged support, he and John Woods hastened to Washington, D.C., to keep Ickes from "making a fool of himself." The secretary, they found, was "quite keen" on moving ahead with Poole's version but agreed to hold off until Oregonians could express their views in detail. Shepard confirmed the widsom of the tactic, and McNary's endorsement undoubtedly contributed to the decision to send Interior representatives to a series of consultations in that state.[11]

Mason made the arrangements for the first meeting, which included ten men who advocated a stronger O&C bill. They agreed that the brief, vague wording should be replaced by "definite controls and objectives." The main issue, Gerlinger told them, was defining the dimensions of sustained-yield management. It was not enough to apply that policy to specific operations; it must be stated as the foundation for administration. Interior's secretaries should have discretion in choosing procedures and making arrangements, but the overall purpose should be mandated by law. As Mason read out the provisions of the De Rouen bill, the members discussed and amended them, thereby transforming the measure from a bureaucratic device into a forestry act. They assured Cordon that such a purpose would also meet the revenue needs of the eighteen O&C counties. The only substantive recommendation they made was to designate half a billion board feet as the annual cut limit until a more accurate timber inventory could be obtained.

The members of the meeting also hoped to commit Interior's secretaries to favor existing operations by owners who practiced forestry methods—a procedural version of Mason's earlier proposals for LCA amendments and the Fletcher bill. The conferees therefore urged the Interior Department to confirm the interests of established and responsible local operators by including a provision for consultation and public hearings. (Interior officials thought these ideas were administrative opinions and certainly not matters for legislative mandate. Instead, Poole inserted a provision empowering officials to reject any bids for O&C timber from lumbermen who did not or would not practice sustained-yield methods themselves.) The conferees then appointed Mason as head of a subcommittee to "whip all these points into shape and draft a bill." Evidently he explained to Shepard the points emphasized by the meeting, because Ickes used those topics soon after in a letter addressed to all Oregonians interested in the legislation.

A few weeks later in mid-July, the Oregon State Planning Board sponsored a meeting of thirty-two persons representing many interests and agencies that would be affected by a new O&C policy. No one from the Interior Department was present this time. Instead, Mason represented the government's role as a continuation of the principles of Article X and the emphases of the Joint Committee. The state board and the Portland chamber committees, he said, recognized that the lumber industry could not adopt those concepts without federal help. Moreover, it was not just a lumberman's bill; the new version would underscore the purpose of securing the economic well-being of dependent communities throughout western Oregon. The harmony Mason sought to bring about with his remarks was somewhat disturbed by Forest Service spokesmen who argued for their agency's jurisdiction over the lands, and by discussion of the counties' revenues issues. Because both issues were "full of political dynamite," Mason feared that they might result in blocking the bill entirely.[12]

The Interior Department called its own meeting in Portland three days afterward. A total of fifty-six, including several who had attended the earlier conferences, heard Poole confirm the department's acceptance of a mandate for forestry as the basis of the O&C administration. Congressman James W. Mott, whose Oregon district included a large portion of the revested lands, insisted that such a gradual, selective harvesting program would soon bankrupt the eighteen counties. How, he asked, could Gerlinger's association support sustained yield without supporting Forest Service jurisdiction? Gerlinger withheld expression of his own doubts about Interior's competence, however. Greeley explained to the group that forest management would in fact build up the value of the timber. Mason warned that it would be unwise to overproduce as a means of taking present advantage of a market that would undoubtedly improve in the future. Most of the participants agreed that the issues of administrative jurisdiction and county payments should be reserved for subsequent legislation. To Mason's relief, no other "fireworks" exploded before the meeting adjourned.

When Poole sent back a draft of the new De Rouen bill to be submitted to the next session of Congress, the Oregonians were pleased to find that it incorporated their substantive if not their procedural recommendations. Mason discussed it with operators in the Eugene area and reported to Poole that they were well satisfied. At a meeting of the WFCA in Portland, however, Allen and Jewett expressed doubts about the government's understanding of the costs to operators involved in sustained yield and wondered whether the bill was another effort to control lumber production. Because of the checkerboard pattern of intermingled ownership of O&C and adjacent lands, Mason recognized that cooperative agreements would in effect extend sustained yield from the public forest to private forests by juxtaposition, not compulsion. His only concern with the new measure was its Title II, which proposed a new and even more complicated formula for county payments.[13]

In view of the administration's recent tendencies, lumbermen had decidedly mixed feelings about the future of their industry, when Roosevelt was overwhelmingly reelected in November 1936. But several larger operators were sufficiently hopeful of the O&C legislation to again finance Mason's return to the nation's capital as lobbyist for that measure. He and his colleagues were, in Gerlinger's words, determined "to see how good a job we can do." Relying on his old network of friendships there, Mason again urged the National Forest Reservation Commission to cultivate lumbermen's participation in the new program.

He also wrote a letter to Silcox, urging him to endorse the bill. Such a stand would certainly be in keeping with the chief's renewed conviction favoring a federal mandate for private forestry. The O&C jurisdictional issue, Mason warned him, was so "loaded with political dynamite" that it could spill over and impede the Forest Service's own interests as contained in the McNary-Doxey bill. It would be "a broad-minded action on your part," he suggested, if the agency would delay suitable settlement of the dispute until a later time. In view of the fact that it had been "a real achievement" to secure agreement on forest management for the much smaller acreage of the O&C lands, it would be wise to take advantage of that precedent. If they did not, he concluded, "I am very much afraid that it may be lost for a number of years to come." When Silcox appeared before the National Forest Reservation Commission in March 1937, he did not challenge Interior's claim to the O&C lands.

In April Mason appeared before De Rouen's committee to defend the practicality of sustained-yield forest management. When some members asked about the higher costs involved, he responded that they were far less than the outlay of private and public funds that would be needed to rescue the economies of dependent communities. To those who worried that only big lumber companies could afford to participate in the cooperative agreements and would thus receive favored status, he gave assurance that smaller operators could be expected to be "very fairly treated" as well.

When the bill was taken up by the House and Senate, the anticipated "fireworks" did not touch on the provisions for sustained yield. Rather, the Forest Service's adherents tried to wrest administrative jurisdiction from Interior by substituting the agency's name throughout the bill at every point where the rival department appeared. Recognizing that the Department of Agriculture had stuck its neck out, Ickes' partisans countered with an amendment that would transfer the Forest Service to Interior—thus employing the Forest Service substitutions to fulfill the secretary's great ambition. At that point, the president intervened in this family feud, and the bill as originally proposed passed handily without further discussion. Roosevelt signed it on August 23, 1937.[14]

Mason was dismayed that Oregon newspapers gave the victory slight notice, but he and his associates nonetheless were greatly pleased. In a letter congratulating Poole on his success at harmonizing conflicting interests, he added an encouraging note: the Hult Lumber Company, one of the smaller operators (a client of Mason's) had already inquired about the process for filing a sustained-yield unit application. Uncertainties and unresolved controversies about access to the O&C lands nevertheless persisited. When the WFCA met in Portland that winter, Allen asked Poole to speak before the conference. The solicitor did so, bringing with him Walter H. Horning, a former professor of forestry who had been working with the National Park Service. They assured the conferees that Interior's General Land Office was committed to the administration's definition of conservation as "prudent use and not hoarding" of natural resources. Horning was impressed with the lumbermen's receptivity toward the financial and technical conditions that would be involved in the new sales contracts, and he advised his superiors to consult continually with them as the regulations were developed. His solicitude and understanding in turn elicited praise from WFCA members and other participants. In a letter to his long-time friend, Lee Muck, now Interior's chief forester, Mason suggested that Horning's diplomatic presentation and ability to work with diverse views were certain grounds for his selection as head of the new O&C Administration.

Secretary Ickes considered several men for the post, including Warren G. Tilton, former Seattle consulting forester and now WCLA executive, and Emanuel Fritz, Mason's aide in the Montana days who was now teaching forestry at Berkeley. Interior officials judged Tilton to be too closely tied with the industry and Fritz as too erratic. As the department's trouble-shooter, Horning himself had the inside lane in the race. Letters of praise from Oregonians representing several viewpoints undoubtedly bolstered his cause.[15]

After Horning was chosen as acting chief forester for the new agency, he submitted a proposal to meet the still unfulfilled desire of the lumbermen who had supported passage of the O&C legislation. It would establish an advisory board as a nongovernmental source of information and assistance to the O&C administrators. The six men named to be its charter members included Gerlinger, Tilton, George W. Peavy, dean of the Oregon State Agricultural College School of Forestry, and Mason, who was named chairman of the group.

Although Horning privately claimed that the initial O&C program was "largely of my contriving," Mason was his principal—and indispensable—advisor. After a decade as harmonizer in the conflicts over forest use, the consultant retained the respect of lumbermen, foresters, and government officials. No man was more knowledgeable about the actual field conditions and statistical dimensions involved in planning management in Oregon forestlands, nor more familiar with the traditional attitudes and practices of lumbermen in the region. Mason's confidence in larger companies, whose financial and technical capacities enabled them to adopt management programs, convinced Horning that he should look to those operators for substantial support. That preference was also determined by terms of the legislation directing Interior to sustain existing enterprises and dependent communities. It was soon confirmed, moreover, when O&C officials reported that smaller companies viewed the sustained-yield terms of O&C contracts as a "hazardous arrangement." As long as there was little competition for O&C timber, that favoritism would remain as a matter of policy.

As chairman of the Advisory Board, Mason rarely interjected his personal opinions into the deliberations. A long-time friend of each of its members, he knew that they shared his own emphases on ensuring the interests of lumbermen who participated in O&C programs. But outside the board's sessions, he worked closely with Horning's deputy, Richard S. Kearns, in formulating a full-scale program for cooperative units in portions of the O&C domain. He had written a management plan for the Hult Lumber Company and now sponsored it as a concrete basis for Kearns' study. The company was a small operation that could offer only 5 percent of the land to be included in a unit, although it planned to purchase additional acreage. The O&C administrators evidently thought it unwise to begin their program in such a small way, and they prolonged consideration of the proposal for several years before dropping it entirely. During that formative period, they were generally satisfied with the results of general sustained-yield practices. The O&C lands became, in Horning's public relations phrase, "one of the nation's largest testing grounds for scientific forest management." However, with the outbreak of World War II, construction demands suddenly increased to meet the needs of mobilization. By 1944 timber sales ensured harvest of over 385 million board feet, worth $1,274,000. Under the circumstances, there was no chance to establish a cooperative program.[6]

7

Another Bears Fruit

Before passage of the O&C Act, George F. Jewett and many other lumbermen had concluded that their industry had very little influence with the New Dealers and that they would therefore have to chart their own course. They considered their own recent record progressive enough, and they felt that the Forest Service's behavior during and after the lumber code period went beyond progressivism to socialism. In 1939, when the Supreme Court upheld the Roosevelt administration's Tennessee Valley Authority, the so-called "yardstick" for water and power production under government control, many lumbermen viewed the decision as an ominous precedent for federal control of their industry as well. Indeed, "if we are going to have a TVA in the lumber business," a Pacific Northwest lumber company owner responded, "I want to get out awfully quick." With characteristic overstatement, Jewett described the federal plan by analogy to the rise of Nazi Germany: a nation embracing socialism in order to cure certain economic evils. "I believe men are more important than trees," he told Ward Shepard. "If we have free men, they will take care of their trees when the time comes."[1]

Advocates of sustained yield viewed the O&C Act as a more encouraging precedent and as a model for legislation that would extend far beyond the western Oregon forests. Forestry programs on the Oregon tracts demonstrated the connection between cooperative arrangements and the economic welfare of those dependent on O&C production. But the national forests included an area and contained stumpage volumes many times larger than the O&C's domain. The predictable need for greater private access to those reserves in the near future would be met, in Mason's words, only through "strong coopera-tion between a progressive industry and a progressive Forest Service."

Although Mason did not intend to ignore his associates' concerns, he refused to let dogmatism destroy opportunity. As in the days of the lumber code, he meant to participate in shaping the government's forestry policy. Centralism, he acknowledged, was a worldwide trend; but he had always believed that its growth in the United States could be made as democratic as possible. Because Chief Silcox was still seeking a federal mandate over the industry, Mason urged the Pacific Northwest Regional Planning Board to call for a congressional study of cooperative management in the national forests. In March 1938 the president included a similar request in his annual message, and Congress soon established the Joint Congressional Committee on Forestry.

Mason hoped that its members would understand the practical basis of the subject; that the industry opposed any federal regulation plan until the government removed the obstacles to public forestry. The committee, he admonished, should also acknowledge the accomplishments by private owners working with little or no encouragement except from state regulations. Finally, assistance should first go to the problem most lumbermen deemed paramount: forest protection.[2]

The Forest Service, however, persisted in its own purpose. It at once submitted to the new committee a "National Forest Cooperative Plan." Silcox had decided that national forest stumpage could be used to promote sustained-yield forestry on intermingled and adjacent private holdings. Ostensibly designed as a means of employing up to half a million farmers and workers still on relief, his proposal would authorize long-term cooperative agreements with selected lumber companies owning timberland adjacent to or intermingled with national forests. Contracts specifying the kinds, amounts, and costs of timber harvested would be administered by state boards of forestry acting as agents for the Forest Service. Silcox's lieutenants subsequently attached two supportive arguments to the program. First, it was the only way of dealing with the increasing migration of operators from Washington State to Oregon. Second, the Forest Service would have to exercise the ultimate decision to break deadlocks that occurred anywhere among private and state parties.[3]

To lumbermen, the idea sounded depressingly familiar. They well remembered what the NRA had done to the industry. Now, they grumbled, New Dealers were contemplating establishing "a local soviet" that would determine every step of production. With unusual bitterness, Mason described the plan as "typical of the New Deal-Forest Service performance." The government was "paying more attention to socializing than to sound forest management." Instead of establishing a forestry program, it used sustained yield as a mere device for unemployment relief. As a result, it would be run by "highly inefficient workers" while the economic burdens of lumbermen were ignored. As for the provision to use state foresters as administrative agents, Mason called it a "sop" to get support from the states. "Sooner or later," he concluded, federal bureaucrats would be in complete control. The plan was thus "a gigantic step toward national regimentation." Much as he had worked with Silcox, Mason was again dismayed by the chief's quest. In the judgment of some who remembered Article X, Silcox was "so volatile" on the matter of federal control, and "so devious" in tactics, that he would try to alter the meaning of the program once it was enacted.[4]

Greeley and Compton tried to soft-pedal the industry's charge of "socialism" during the hearings of the Joint Congressional Committee. But the old specter of government domination haunted the new effort to establish a harmonious cooperative program. Yet, in spite of attempts by a few legislators to refight the old lumber code debate, Mason found surprising support for sustained yield. Lumbermen still doubted the economic flexibility of cooperative units, but Mason believed that they would be willing to go along with gradually developed state regulation in limited areas. Then, when the Forest Service offered reasonable terms for cooperative management in the national forests, a majority of owners would agree to those arrangements. Mason still counted on the larger companies to point the way. A spokesman for one of them proudly proclaimed that tree farming had been the industry's aim ever since it "undertook to handle the forestry problem" after the collapse of NRA. As on previous occasions, Mason now guided members of the congressional committee to the best examples of private-public forest management in the Pacific Northwest. One of the sites, Weyerhaeuser's White River forestry unit, consisted of 58 percent company land, 38 percent national forest, and 8 percent state tracts.

Greeley supported Mason's argument that the industry had been promoting cooperative forestry for years. He hailed the White River unit and other projects as "the real stuff—with long-term plans for building up growing stock and converting the enterprise over to sustained yield."[5] He told the Joint Congressional Committee that his own WCLA had recently cooperated with the Pacific Northwest Loggers Association (later reorganized as the Industrial Forestry Association) to form a Joint Committee on Forest Conservation. Together with the Pacific Northwest Loggers Association, the WCLA had employed foresters as inspectors, written a handbook of forest practices, and coordinated these activities with the state foresters.[6]

Mason's forest resources report particularly impressed Governor Charles A. Sprague of Oregon. Fearing that his state would become a "tributary colony" if the Forest Service's plan was adopted, Sprague asked the legislature to approve a full-scale program of cutting, planting, and protection of state forests through joint agreements with lumbermen. He also launched a "Keep Oregon Green" publicity program to educate the citizenry on the subject of forest fire prevention. Mason acted as liaison to the Portland Chamber of Commerce and Regional Planning Board. State and civic officials welcomed the cooperation of the Forest Service in these programs, especially its acquisition of cutover lands that companies could not or would not replant.[7]

Aware of the attitudes and ambitions of various administration officials, some lumbermen still regarded cooperative sustained yield as "Silcox's baby" and suspected it was a subterfuge for federal control. (When the Forest Service later publicized Weyerhaeuser's tree farms, as if finally acknowledging the existence of private forestry, few lumbermen were willing to conclude that the agency had undergone a change of heart.) Just as the Joint Congressional Committee began hearings on a cooperative program in December 1939, Silcox died. Another of Mason's old mentors, Earle H. Clapp, was appointed as acting chief. Clapp shared his predecessor's belief in federal management of private forestlands, but lacked equal influence. Indeed, his pronouncements succeeded only in further alienating the lumber industry.[8]

In March 1941 the Joint Congressional Committee endorsed cooperative agreements for the national forests. Senator McNary introduced a cooperative sustained-yield forestry bill, but lumbermen found the proposal far from satisfactory. Some thought that a few operators might find attractive features in it, but most felt that it gave too much federal control for private property for long periods of time.[9]

As the national defense emergency developed during 1940 and 1941, there was little chance for reconsideration of the bill, but McNary continued to introduce it in each successive Congress. Its advocates subsequently were encouraged by several events. The first of these was the November 1942 election that gave the Republican party greater power in both houses of Congress. The second was the appointment, soon after, of Lyle F. Watts as chief of the Forest Service. When Watts had been regional forester in Portland, Mason and many lumbermen had found him to be more approachable than his superiors. When the new chief indicated to them that he was ready "to get on a better footing with the industry," NLMA leaders decided that their members should take advantage of the change. Watts was, one later remarked, "the type to get out and sell tree farming to the cold, practical-minded businessman."[10]

The most encouraging sign that the time for forestry legislation had arrived came from several large lumber companies. Acting through their trade associations, they proposed to hire a lobbyist to make certain that the McNary measure would truly establish an equal basis for cooperative agreements in the national forests. The small group of advocates, including Mason, Jewett, Greeley, NLMA foresters G. Harris Collingwood and Wellington Burt, and Arizona lumberman James G. McNary, had been discussing strategy for more than two years. Now they were ready to act. Mason's colleagues at first considered hiring a professional lobbyist, but they soon agreed that Mason was "probably the best man for the job" in view of his experience, his network of friendships, and the confidence he inspired among both lumbermen and officials. "I believe that I am just as well equipped as anyone else," Mason replied to their invitation. As he prepared to depart once again for Washington, D.C., in January 1943, Greeley warned him not to let himself be "tagged" as a representative of business or he would come under attack from prejudiced New Dealers.[11]

Mason did not need advice about lobbying tactics. Although some of his supporters hoped that the job could be finished within four months, he himself estimated that it would take twice that time just to prepare strategy. The omnibus approach of the Fletcher and McNary-Doxey bills would have to be abandoned. The advocates of cooperative forestry, he felt, should minimize risks and maximize the chances for success by advancing three separate measures. One would extend Clarke-McNary Act payments, another would establish a yield tax, and the third would authorize federal forestry agencies to make sustained-yield units and cooperative agreements. Because traditional jealousy between Agriculture and Interior was just then exacerbated by a controversy over the O&C indemnity lands, Mason urged McNary to include Interior Secretary Ickes' department in the authorization. The amendment would replace the O&C Act's provision for rejecting non-sustained-yield sale bids with a positive requirement. When Ickes supported the bill, McNary was pleasantly surprised. Collingwood described it as a proper addition to Mason's "laurels."

The Forest Service demonstrated its enthusiasm by assigning eight staff members to design a draft that would attract the broadest participation and support. Their chairman was Assistant Chief Raymond E. Marsh, who had worked with Mason during the LCA period. Interior's counterpart in interdepartmental conferences on the bill was another old friend, Lee Muck. Shuffling back and forth from Agriculture to Interior and lunching with Watts, Compton, and others, Mason helped "make all of the many wheels go faster." Together with Collingwood, he also overcame the Bureau of Budget's initial opposition to the sustained-yield measure. In frequent conferences with McNary, he drafted amendments and polished the language of the bill, and, at the Senate Interior Committee's hearings, he pointed out the extent to which the industry was committed to forest management on a cooperative basis. The clients of his own consulting firm, for example, had already devoted 875,000 acres to such programs. Predicting that the bill would be favorably reported by the committee, McNary promised him that "hell and high water will not prevent it going through the House."

Neither of those forces made an appearance, but lesser problems were troublesome enough. Like some undying spirit of the past, Gifford Pinchot publicly criticized his own child, the Forest Service. Its professed concern for constitutionality and democracy embodied in cooperative forestry, he declared, was nothing but a cover for its new-found solicitude for lumbermen. When Ovid Butler responded with a defense of industrial forestry, Pinchot answered that the AFA and SAF supported sustained yield only when it was profitable for foresters and operators. AFA's president, William S. Rosecrans, chose to avoid public controversy, but in private he asserted that there was no need for complete federal control of operators as advocated by Pinchot, because the police powers of the state were sufficient enough to guard the public interest in lumbering. In private correspondence, Mason tactfully assured Oregonians that there was no political maneuvering involved in the Forest Service's support of the bill. But the Oregon Board of Forestry wondered whether the federal program would supesede its own authority given by the legislation of the Sprague administration.

Ignoring these objections, McNary "drove" the sustained-yield measure through the Senate "like a fire engine going down Second Avenue," as Greeley described it. It then came to rest at "dead center" in the House. Mason, who had been in Portland for several months, returned to the nation's capital in September 1943. When he called on Hampton P. Fulmer, chairman of the House Agriculture Committee, he found the South Carolina congressman highly skeptical of the bill and inclined to delay consideration of it. Because of Fulmer's subsequent absences, however, Oregon Republican Lowell Stockman eventually secured committee approval of the Senate's version.[12]

In January 1944 the bill was taken off the House calendar. Because that was an election year, its advocates concentrated their efforts on Oregon Senator Rufus C. Holman. The senator had been critical of forestry proposals a few years before but was now seeking reelection and was eager to share credit for the measure. In February, however, chances for passage of the sustained-yield bill were endangered by President Roosevelt's veto of an amendment to the Internal Revenue Code that would have instituted a capital gains tax on timber appreciation. Speaking as a grower and seller of timber, he told the Congress that he favored treating timber as a crop, taxing the gain as an ordinary annual gain rather than as a capital gain. Mason at once sent out telegrams "to combat" the "inaccurate" statement, and Holman inserted the counterargument into the *Congressional Record*. That was hardly effective, but three days later Congress overrode the veto, and the tax became Section 631 of the Internal Revenue Code. The exultation of its supporters was suddenly cut short, however, when on February 25, Senator McNary died. One of the last things their old champion had read was Mason's letter discusing further strategy for passage of the sustained-yield bill.

McNary's appointed successor was Douglas County attorney Guy Cordon, Mason's colleague on the O&C Advisory Board and a firm believer in cooperative forestry as an asset to the lumber industry and to dependent communities. In March Cordon urged his fellow senators to pass the bill as a memorial to McNary. His effort was aided in the House by M. Harris Ellsworth, whose Oregon district contained more timber than the constituency of any other congressman. Ellsworth proceeded to work "a kind of hocus-pocus," Mason reported. When another member offered further objections to consideration of the measure, Ellsworth called down Mason, Collingwood, Burt, and Muck from the House gallery to draft an amendment to satisfy the critic. Then he asked for a voice vote on the bill. Speaker Sam T. Rayburn thought that a very irregular procedure but agreed to it. The cooperative sustained-yield authority was duly passed; this time the president cast no veto.

The act, now designated as Public Law 273, embodied the long hoped-for concept of joint federal-industry cooperation in the form of a contract in which each side shared responsibilities and profits. Like the O&C Act of 1937, its primary purpose was to maintain dependent communities. For Mason, it was "like a dream which finally turns out all right." Back in Portland, he returned to a desk heaped with congratulations. The expense account he submitted to his sponsors asked for $7,373.69 for his work from the fall of 1941 to the end of March 1944. Of that sum, only $4,900 was paid to him during the subsequent period, but nowhere in the champion lobbyist's correspondence or diary was there a word of impatience or complaint.[13]

Within a month after passage of PL 273, Mason set to work to prepare proposals for its implementation in the Pacific Northwest. Now in his sixties, he retained the vigor and purpose that had characterized his efforts over more than two decades of crusading. He and his associates in forestry and lumbering had been planning for postwar opportunities as early as 1942. When the war ended in 1945, economic conditions seemed most propitious. Severe overcutting had left great tracts of land suitable for second growth. While the volume of available private timber had diminished, a housing boom boosted the prices for lumber. Lumbermen could therefore see that access to the public forests was not only essential but increasingly profitable. Even smaller-sized companies could now secure credits and exchanges to qualify for participation in cooperative agreements. The principal difficulty was Mason's own: it would be "quite a bit of a job and a long-winded affair" to design sustained-yield projects. But he soon had a half dozen ready for submission.

One of these proposals involved William E. Boeing, lumberman turned aircraft magnate who owned 16,000 acres of timber. Mason explained to him that a sustained-yield management program would ultimately be more profitable than merely holding the property as an investment. The businessman did not follow up on the idea, however. Another proposal would provide the C. D. Johnson Lumber Company of Lincoln County, Oregon, with "a most unusual opportunity" to become "one of the very best demonstrations of a sustained-yield unit in the western United States." Because its holdings included a variety of forest types as well as stands of old-growth timber and the only mill in the area, the company needed to do nothing more than secure additional acreage. Its board of directors agreed to devote capital gains and depletion income to the project and instructed Mason to "get a foot in the door" of the federal forestry agencies. Unable to accomplish that familiar feat, Mason asked Senator Cordon to help another possible project: Mason's newly redesigned plan for Brooks Scanlon Lumber Company in Bend, Oregon. The influential Bend editor and conservationist, Robert W. Sawyer, supported the idea, but the proposal remained just that.[14]

The most promising—and impressive—project Mason developed was the Hill Properties. Those acreages resembled the O&C checkerboard; they originated in a land grant of alternate sections six miles on both sides of a wagon road route across Deschutes, Jefferson, and Linn counties in Oregon's Willamette River valley. Although emigrant and commercial traffic reached a height in the 1890s, little settlement remained in the area. The road company's land patents were subsequently purchased by an investment company whose stockholders included Louis W. Hill, son of James J. Hill, the famous "Empire Builder" of the Great Northern Railway. When the property was eventually divided, Hill elected to retain the timbered two-thirds (123,000 acres) of the total.

In April 1937, amid the turmoil of the O&C legislative campaign, Hill's agent, the First Trust Company of St. Paul, Minnesota, hired Mason to evaluate the holdings. At the time, Hill contemplated no forestry program. (Perhaps that idea seemed irreconcilable with the hostile attitude toward forest conservation he had formed during the days of Pinchot's tenure at the Forest Service.) Hill's agent, therefore, warned Mason not to emphasize forest management in his reports. Instead, the consultant quietly worked away while other conditions developed that would bolster his subsequent recommendations. During the years when sales remained desultory and income minimal, the company blocked up the checkerboard ownership by purchases and exchanges with private, state, and federal ownerships, until the Hill Properties consisted primarily of a 145,000-acre timberland tract, most of it in Linn County.

Although Mason kept his forestry ideas to himself, the company's executives saw that Weyerhaeuser and Crown Zellerbach tree farms in adjacent areas were demonstrating the practical possibilities of sustained-yield projects. "Well, Mason," Hill remarked, "you know more about this than any of the rest." Eventually Hill approved the manager's proposal for employing similar methods on a limited basis but emphasized that the program would be subordinated to timber sales. Just before the war, Mason also launched a program to educate the owners about methods of investing in seeding, replanting, and other silvicultural treatments. By 1945, after state and federal legislation enhanced the economic benefits involved, the Hill executives agreed to a full management program for their property. In effect Mason had created an exemplary sustained-yield unit. In 1946 he successfully promoted a long-term timber sale agreement with Willamette Valley lumbermen William Swindells (Gerlinger's son-in-law), Fred Powers, and Carl Davis to take advantage of the new plywood market. Soon after, he recommended the formation of "Hill Forests, Inc.," as an entity for cooperative agreements with federal agencies under PL 273.[15]

Federal foresters welcomed all of Mason's proposals, but their own plans took precedence. At Interior, Richard Kearns' O&C prospectus of 1939 was rearranged to fit a much larger program. Learning that Horning envisioned esablishment of about twenty units on the O&C lands, Greeley happily described them from the industry's viewpoint as "the meat in the coconut." In order to hold public hearings on them in November 1944, the General Land Office urged Ickes' deputy, Undersecretary Oscar A. Chapman, to proceed with the program. When other advisers secured a delay of several months, Mason used that period to work out details that were sure to be raised at the hearings. By broadening the scope of the program, he hoped to give to owners not participating in specific units incentives to employ sustained-yield practices in their operations.

When the O&C officials proposed the first Sustained Yield Unit—the Siuslaw—in Lane and Linn counties in March 1945, many area lumbermen objected to it. About eighty smaller companies in Oregon immediately organized the Western Association of Loggers and Lumber-

men. Its acronym, WALL, revealed its purpose: to stop what the
lumbermen viewed as federal authorization of a monopoly by larger
operators. The unit agreement would grant to seven companies owning
58 percent of the timberlands a hundred-year contract giving them exclusive access to the timber on the O&C lands intermingled with their own.
Several of these enterprises were or had been Mason's clients and had
been favored by Horning's sales policy during the war. Although Ickes
did not like monopolies by private capital, he approved of the project
as most protective of the public interest. But early in 1946, he resigned
his office—"with a loud bang," as Mason recorded.[16]

The new Interior secretary, Julius Krug, had slight knowledge of
forestry apart from the briefs Chapman gave him. While his lieutenants
reorganized the General Land Office into the Bureau of Land Management (BLM), consideration of the Siuslaw proposal was delayed
further. Moreover, the political and economic climates had changed
significantly since the O&C administrators first conceived of their
program. Having regained control of Congress, Republicans launched a
campaign to discredit and overturn the legacies of the New Deal, now
guarded by the Harry S Truman administration. Natural resources
policy was a favorite target. In addition, the number of lumbermen in
Oregon had proliferated to meet wartime and postwar demands and
prices.

In 1937 there were 46 companies operating in Lane County; by 1946
there were 208. In adjacent Linn County, those totals were 30 and 103
respectively. Instead of the 30 percent reduction in private forest owners
that Walter Horning anticipated, the O&C Administration was faced
with a situation in which H.J. Cox, executive secretary of the Willamette
Valley Lumbermen's Association, observed, "neither the Interior
Department nor Houdini (if alive)" could dole out timber to every
company and still carry out the intent of the O&C Act of 1937.

WALL's continuing opposition campaign promoted second thoughts
among many lumbermen about the O&C Administration's proposal.
When Frank Reid, leader of the organization, told Oregon's congressional delegation that larger lumber companies were responsible for the
lumber shortage that was limiting the postwar housing boom, Senator
Cordon urged Interior's foresters to find some place in their program
for "a reasonable number of small operators" employing good cutting
and utilization methods. But lumbermen operating on the O&C lands
actually wanted an absolute monopoly for cooperators, with several
further concessions attached. Some found the terms of the agreements
"rather stiff." Others wanted better assurance about the quality of the
timber sold and cost estimates in order to plan their purchases
accurately. None liked the idea of participating in a managed unit if a

portion of it was made available to small contractors, generally called "gyppos." Supporters of cooperative units considered the issue "too important to the West to allow it to go by default." Noting that Oregon newspapers were giving no coverage to their side of the controversy, they discussed ways of offsetting WALL's "insidious" misrepresentations.

Mason did not apparently notice the implications of such "grassroots" opposition. His attitude was, however, consistent with his confidence in large lumber companies. He expressed disappointment when the O&C Advisory Board did not give the matter sufficient attention and likened the crisis to the League of Nation's failure to act against aggressors during the 1930's. As he had done with his "Brakes" paper twenty years before, he now sent a lengthy memorandum to his associates. The industry, he argued, must mount an educational campaign pointing out that the cooperative agreements were advantageous to all parties.

Some WCLA members worried that taking sides would jeopardize financial support for their organization, but Greeley supported Mason's idea. Sustained yield, he added, should be explained not as a practice imposed from above but as "a current forestry development" taking place through the initiative of lumbermen themselves. In June 1946 he personally contributed to the educational campaign by giving a speech defending industrial forestry. About the same time, Horning used Mason's arguments to charge that WALL's alternative "merit system" for access to public timber was "in reality a plan of unlimited exploitation" of that resource.[17]

As long as the controversy raged, the Interior Department would not allow the O&C administrators to proceed with their Siuslaw proposal. The Forest Service was not similarly bound, however. Its Region Six officials urged Oregon lumbermen to enter into sustained-yield programs in order to escape the fate of their forebearers in the timber-depleted states of the East. Six months after PL 273 went on the *Federal Register*, over a hundred applications came into the agency's offices—forty of them to the Portland desk alone. Chief Watts and his assistants nevertheless decided to "go slow" in establishing their program in order to protect the public interest. At the outset, they planned to create no more than one or two units in each national forest district, with more in the West where there were fewer operators with whom contracts would have to be negotiated.

Mason was the only nonagency person invited to their preliminary deliberations. As always he was ready with several proposals. One, for the Truckee River in northern California, involved forestland that the Southern Pacific Railroad would otherwise liquidate. A second combined national forest land with the holdings of Mason's long-time client, Shevlin-Hixon Lumber Company of Bend, Oregon. But editor Robert Sawyer, head of the Bend Chamber of Commerce, raised the question of possible exclusion of other local lumbermen from the area's forests. The Forest Service officials rejected Mason's proposal, partly because they did not agree with Hixon's demand for mandatory arbitration of disputes in carrying out contract terms. Impressed by Interior's problems with WALL, they also did not want to become entangled in the controversy over monopoly. They did, however, find "some very real advantages" for both sides in Mason's plan for a cooperative agreement with Hill Properties. Unfortunately, executives of that company evidently declined to press for confirmation of the proposal.

In its Pacific Northwest region, the Forest Service had begun an analysis of potential cooperative units soon after passage of PL 273. But owners of timberland in western Washington presented the agency with an initial plan. Weyerhaeuser had long considered expanding its tree farm in that quarter of the Olympic Peninsula. In 1943 Greeley proposed a cooperative plan that would include the Quinault Indian Reservation and state forests. George Cornwall of the *Timberman* and George L. Drake of Simpson Timber Company had conceived of a project in the area several years before anyone else. Now, two of Mason's long-time associates, H. J. Andrews of the Forest Service and Simpson's Chrysogonus H. Kreienbaum at Shelton on the peninsula, worked for an arrangement that would reduce the amount of damage involved in harvest operations and reforest cutover lands.

Because Simpson held nearly 60 percent of the total included in the planned cooperative units, the Forest Service recognized that it would not raise the issue of competition between big and small operators. And since it was explicitly designed to sustain the economies of Shelton and other nearby mill towns, the proposal was enthusiastically endorsed by labor and commercial organizations in the area. Although some lumbermen privately predicted that the company would "lose its identity as part of a free enterprise system," others noted that it would obtain access to four times as much timber as it already owned. In all, the public hearings on the proposed "Federal Unit" were a happy contrast to the contentious meetings on the O&C Administration's Siuslaw plan. The Forest Service-Simpson contract was soon after signed and the unit was established on December 12, 1946.[18]

8
Deliberate Pruning

Creation of the Shelton Cooperative Sustained Yield Unit did not break the stalemate in implementing PL 273, as the proponents of that legislation expected. Instead, the idea behind the authority proved to be one whose time had evidently passed. Cooperation between private and public sectors of the economy had been desirable and often essential during the years of depression, recovery, and war. By 1947, however, new economic and political opportunities produced a climate in which many businessmen viewed cooperation as unnecessary and even subversive. Members of the lumber industry generally held that view— indeed, they always had. Officials of the Truman administration hoped that they could overcome the dilemma involved. But those in both camps who believed that cooperative forestry was mutually beneficial were a minority whose former influence was eroded by the new climate of opinion.

The Forest Service's plans at Shelton had prompted the Interior Department to create a dozen master units for administration of the O&C lands. Several of them were designed to contain cooperative units. Anticipating substantial support, Mason noted that of the fifty units that might be established, he himself would be interested in twenty-five; indeed, twelve of those would engage lumbermen who were already his clients.

Walter Horning submitted the first proposal to his immediate superior, C. Girard Davidson, assistant secretary for land management and Krug's principal adviser on the subject. The O&C forester had made a tentative agreement with the Fischer Lumber Company of Marcola, near Eugene, to participate in sustained-yield cutting along the Mohawk River in Lane and Linn counties. According to Mason's analysis, it was superior to the Forest Service's arrangement because the cooperator would participate in determining the allowable cut over a longer period of time and would have no competition in access to the public forests. The Forest Service had declined to participate in an earlier proposal; this plan would encompass only private and BLM lands. Mindfull of WALL's opposition and of the Shelton solution, Horning had selected a company of medium size as the sole participant in the contract. To qualify for confirmation, Fischer would have to acquire additional acreage and agree to reciprocal road rights and financial liability.[1]

Anxious to catch up with the Forest Service's lead, Horning began publicizing "the Promised Land" of cooperative sustained-yield units. He did not, however, refer to local public opinion when he announced the plan. Davidson's friends in Oregon quickly warned the assistant secretary that the contract would have political repercussions. As a result, Davidson viewed the O&C administrator's actions as an example of "government by fluke" and decided to go to Eugene to conduct public hearings on the Fischer-Mohawk Unit. When he arrived there in January 1948, he consulted with Mason. Both agreed that it was a "bad time and place" to hold a debate on "a proposal to dedicate certain public timber to operation by a single sawmill," but Mason felt that his reputation and experience would carry substantial weight with the large audience. Mason described the plan as "feasible and workable," and, referring to federal flood control efforts in the region, predicted that it would help control "floods of timber" then glutting the market as a response to all-time high prices. Aware of the political views of his associates, he added that the arrangement was neither rigid nor compulsory; it would not involve "sovietizing everything."

Unimpressed with the speaker's background, WALL's leaders roundly denounced the Fischer contract and another BLM proposed unit in Montana. As a more proper alternative, they called for federal subsidy for any practitioner of sustained yield whenever voters in the affected area approved of the contracts. After the Eugene hearing, WALL held a series of rallies in several other western Oregon mill towns. Mason considered the organization's presentation "a highly skilled piece of demagoguery," but its arguments obviously appealed to those who believed competition was the source of increased production, jobs, and the general welfare of communities and counties.[2]

Keenly aware of the potential damage the Fischer-Mohawk issue might do to the administration's far more important resource programs and to the Democrats' chances in the 1948 election, Davidson directed his right-hand man, Daniel Goldy, to overhaul not only Horning's proposal but the entire sustained-yield management policy for the O&C lands. Long-term contracts would now be subject to periodic review and revisions. But cooperative agreements within specific units were relegated to the status of an option. Thereafter, the practice of forestry

methods would be assured by regulating reciprocal access-road contracts, to be made with qualified operators of any size.

While his superiors were trying to prevent the issue from dividing
local operators, Horning himself widened the breach. In a private
meeting with lumbermen whom he had previously favored in O&C
sales, he expressed doubts about the effectiveness of the new policy. It
would, he felt, give a free hand to "gyppos" and eviscerate the unit
program. Richard Kearns described it as "a stew." Within a few
months, Horning was transferred back to the Washington, D.C., office
and was succeeded by Goldy. Kearns subsequently resigned his federal
post and took his talents to Mason's consulting firm.

Although Republicans in Congress were mollified by Davidson's
statements, the Senate Interior Committee came to Oregon a few
months later to hold hearings on the administration's forest policies.
After seeking permission to address their session in Eugene, Mason
presented something of a personal statement. In it he recapitulated the
history of his sustained-yield crusade from his "Brakes" paper, to the
TCB and Article X of the lumber code, to the forest advisory
committees of the state and region, and finally the passage of PL 273.
Mere forestry practices could not maintain dependent communities, he
concluded; only long-term cooperative agreements could do that.
Admitting that he had clients who might benefit from such contracts, he
pointed out that his work with the Hill Properties confirmed his lifelong conviction that only larger companies could bear the expense of
participating in those agreements. The senators must understand, he
said, that these enterprises would be making another kind of contribution: they would be giving up their "freedom of action" over a period of
many years. That was a paramount consideration for those who
remembered the days of the NRA. Cooperative contracts were not a
complete answer to the complex problems of the lumber market, but he
thought they were "the most adequate solution."[3]

Mason's statement was something of a farewell address. As part of
O&C's new policy, the Advisory Board was reorganized to include the
widest scope of viewpoints, representing community interests as well as
those of the industry. As the latter's advocate, Mason had served for a
decade; now, with change so obviously in the air, he was ready to step
down. (It is possible, of course, that the new Interior officials were not
comfortable with what was now viewed as a conflict of interest: Mason's
continuing work for many established lumber companies.) At the
board's meeting that same September, he endorsed the nomination of
former governor Charles A. Sprague to be his successor as chairman.
With a bonus from Hill executives larger than his annual income had
ever been, he took a refreshing trip to Hawaii a few months later.

Although Mason viewed Goldy's "hard-boiled" road agreements as demanding too much of operators without sufficient reciprocity, he continued to work with the federal policymakers, just as he had done after the collapse of NRA and the impasse over sustained-yield legislation. Privately, he shared the hopes of his trade associates that a Republican victory that November would bring a more resolute team of administrators to the Interior Department. They thought that Congressman Harris Ellsworth would be the best choice for secretary; Senator Guy Cordon was also mentioned for that post. After the Truman administration won a second term, however, federal foresters did not dispense with Mason's expertise. He returned to the Advisory Board and, as chairman of its access road subcommittee, he helped design the details of road and right-of-way contracts that were now central to sustained-yield management on those lands.

Although he found the Shelton Unit going "beautifully," Mason was unable to extract other cooperative agreements from the mire of controversy. The Fischer-Mohawk contract was blocked by political backbiting—marked by the resignation of Goldy and his chief, BLM Director Marion Clawson—within the Interior Department. The lumber company's outspoken owner adamantly presented demands of his own. With Kearns' help, Mason designed other proposals for submission to the Forest Service but could not overcome lumbermen's distrust of that agency. Indeed, Mason himself found its road and logging requirements unacceptable for the Hill Properties.[4]

Perhaps to demonstrate an ongoing commitment to the cooperative basis for forestry, the Forest Service established several more "Federal Units"—its own version of Interior's sustained-yield units. Judging that the southwest Washington area could support such an operation, the agency started one in Grays Harbor County in 1949. A smaller program was begun in New Mexico, but when another larger one was proposed for the Fremont National Forest on the southern border of Oregon, the details quickly aroused a controversy that had to be resolved by Congress and the secretary of agriculture.[5]

Many members of the industry had been looking forward for some time to the coming of a Republican administration and an end to what some called the "present trend toward socializing all parts of the economy." Still publicizing the "great progress" being made in private forestry practices, Mason declared himself "hell-bent against federal regulation in the forests of the country." Along with his associates, he thought he had shocking proof of that tendency in 1949 when New Mexico Senator Clinton P. Anderson, former secretary of agriculture, introduced a bill to extend such regulation to private forests. The Industrial Forestry Association's William D. Hagenstein concluded that the government's effort "is probably always going to be with us." For his part, Mason decided that the likelihood cast a shadow on his hopes for more cooperative units. That same year, his plan for a three-way agreement (Hill-Forest Service-O&C) expired amid mutual concern for public support.[6]

In 1952 the Republican party offered a change from what it claimed were two decades of Democratic centralism and control of business. When its presidential candidate, Dwight D. Eisenhower, spoke in Portland during the campaign, Mason was delighted by his call for "partnership" in resource development generally and an end to corruption in the management of Indian timber specifically. Paradoxically, however, cooperative forestry fell victim to the business-oriented officials of the Republican administration, who pared the budgets and the authority of both the Interior and Agriculture departments.

Interior was now under the nominal direction of former Oregon governor Douglas McKay, a friend of the lumber industry. Greeley hailed his appointment as a restoration of the balance between federal and state, and private and public interests. But when Interior ordered changes in O&C policies, even the critics of Goldy acknowledged how effective and lucrative those policies had already become. Mason attended long and contentious sessions of the Advisory Board in order to facilitate department revision of the access road regulations. But the only substantial policy change subsequently adopted was an increase in the allowable cut.

Two other good intentions similarly led to a morass of controversy. First, Republicans hoped that the termination of Indian reservations would facilitate better management of tribal timberlands, but they found that some Indian owners were far more interested in immediate income. Second, the new BLM officials meant to confirm the Fischer-Mohawk contract solely as a business obligation; they were soon being charged with favoritism and monopoly. Like their predecessors, they gingerly backed away from the issue. There was one positive note, however. Under orders from the real policymakers in the White House, Interior's foresters brought their programs in line with those in Agriculture. BLM reassessed the efficacy of its policy of limiting sales to mills in areas adjacent to the timber harvested (marketing areas) and, after a stormy hearing in Portland, announced that these would be ended. In turn, the Forest Service agreed to practice the more stringent forestry techniques used by the BLM. In all, the agreements amounted to a remarkable change in the antipathies of earlier years.

While accomplishing little in the way of concrete benefits for the industry, the Eisenhower administration gratified lumbermen generally by retaining Richard E. McArdle as chief of the Forest Service, even though he was a Democratic appointee. (Mason had known and admired him for years and had once tried to bring him into the partnership.) The chief confirmed his own opposition to any attempts to extend federal authority over private forests. That meant, however, that his agency would establish no more cooperative sustained-yield units.[7]

Ever since the controversy over the Fremont National Forest proposal four years before, the Forest Service had questioned the wisdom and desirability of extending their activities under PL 273. In 1954, when the Grays Harbor operation was judged to have made "an effective contribution" to the local economy, another agreement was planned for the same region. It would include portions of the Gifford Pinchot National Forest and the holdings of the Weyerhaeuser Timber Company near Mt. St. Helens. Lumbermen and civic leaders in nearby Vancouver, Washington, immediately objected to its exclusive terms. Only a few companies seemed willing to have the secretary of agriculture in effect sitting as a member of their board of directors. The Forest Service therefore decided to secure sustained-yield practices through cutting and sales contracts and by administering them not in special units but within traditional "working circles."

Without referring to the obvious recurring political controversies that had marred the cooperative unit proposals, McArdle's office issued a declaration in 1956 describing the federal unit as a concept "of questionable value." There were many alternative combinations of management arrangements that could accomplish the purposes of PL 273 without involving the government in controversies. Promising to maintain the five existing units, the chief asked Congress to repeal the Forest Service's authority under that law. After Democrats reassumed control of Congress in 1957, Oregon's Senator Richard L. Neuberger, a champion of the Forest Service, joined James A. Murray of Montana, chairman of the Senate Interior Committee, to introduce a repeal bill. The move, which was roundly debated by such organizations as the American Forestry Association and the Industrial Forestry Association, never came to a vote. In 1963 national and regional organizations were also instrumental in securing an executive directive from the secretary of agriculture applying as overall policy for sustained-yield forestry practices in national forests for the purpose of sustaining dependent communities—the fundamental provision of the acts of 1937 and 1944.[8]

Though they had fought long and hard for legislative authority for cooperative forestry, Mason and other advocates evidently saw no reason to lament the demise of federal initiatives. For some, it was not so much a matter of clashing political philosophies as it was simply too many complications. Weyerhaeuser officials were proud that the lumber industry had "embraced forestry in spite of the 'Great Crusade'" by the

Portrait of Mason by Bruce Bomberger, used by the Weyerhaeuser Company in an advertising series. Mason was referred to as the "father of sustained-yield forestry."

Mason in one of many interview sessions with Elwood R. Maunder, executive director of the Forest History Society, ca. 1968.

"Mr. Sustained Yield" and "Mr. Douglas-fir." Mason recalls earlier challenges with Leo A. Isaac, who spent a long research career with the Forest Service and wrote many important papers about Douglas-fir.

A. A. Heckman, executive director of the Louis W. and Maud Hill Family Foundation (now Northwest Area Foundation), and Mason confer in 1962.

Evelyn and David Mason depart New York for a European vacation, 1950.

David T. Mason, 1958.

ideological heirs of Pinchot. Self-enforcement of Article X by WCLA members, for example, had become a permanent requirement administered by four full-time foresters as field investigators. Western Oregon lumbermen were satisfied by the fact that timber production in their area had increased two and a half times between 1925 and 1951. Members of Mason's old organization, the Western Pine Association, had established 363 of their own cooperative units containing 4.5 million acres. By 1952 there were 3,541 tree farms in thirty-three states containing 24.8 million acres. In 1954 alone, Weyerhaeuser's fourteen tree farms produced nearly 50 million board feet of timber. Mason's greatest source of personal satisfaction came from his management of the Hill Properties, now called Timber Service Company. In a few years, he observed, it had "changed from lots of timber with [a] small demand at low prices to [a] shortage of timber, great demand and at high prices." Its production of nearly 1.5 billion board feet in the mid-1950s sold at an average price of about $8.00 per thousand. Public timber at that same time, he recorded in his diary, was going for only $5.50 per thousand. The genetic seed orchard serving the property was subsequently named in his honor.[9]

In a larger context, several factors combined to account for foresters' and lumbermen's confidence. A majority of operators employed on-going, often long-term and—most importantly—flexible growing and harvesting practices involving every kind of ownership pattern. Mason ascribed the "excellent progress" made by these lumbermen not to PL 273, but to the capital gains taxation measure he had lobbied for at the same time. Section 631 of the Internal Revenue Code and the adoption of allowable limits, he estimated, had laid the foundation for 80 percent of the forest management programs applied to private lands. But the state should adopt similar provisions: "To my mind," he told Charles Sprague in 1959, "the greatest threat to private forestry today here in Oregon is taxation." Later, when Congress considered a bill altering Section 631, Mason warned that the bill would relegate timber to second class citizenship among other kinds of assets and destroy future potentials for forest management on private lands.[10]

It was obvious from this latter-day crusade that the veteran forester was not about to retire. He continued to assist clients in the mergers that were once again changing the dimensions of the industry and its market. As elder statesman of his partnership, he counseled associates on a variety of projects to increase volume and profit. In other matters, he acted as "father" to new leaders of the industry. In active pursuit of all of these tasks, he sometimes hiked through second-growth stands, many of which he had first seen as barren, cutover tracts earlier in the century.

Whenever he was in Washington, D.C., he called on his old friends in the federal forestry agencies, joining in their reminiscences, awarding "roses" to some figures of the past, and "skunk cabbage" to others—again, characteristically declining to name names. Back at Berkeley, he lectured to a class about the opportunities available in industrial forestry—and found the students' response as disappointing as it had been when he left there in 1921. In Salem, Oregon, he helped celebrate the twentieth and silver anniversaries of the passage of the O&C Act. Expanding the scope and comparisons of his earlier calculations, he traveled to observe forestry practices in light of new priorities for recreation, wildlife, and population, not only in the United States, but also in Europe, South America, Asia, and the South Pacific.

About the time he was completing his official service with the O&C Advisory Board, he started on the beginnings of quite a different kind of legacy. At the behest of Rodney C. Loehr of the University of Minnesota, he prepared a statement on the place of cooperative sustained-yield management in American forest history. Learning of the volumes of diaries Mason had kept, Loehr suggested that relevant extracts be published to document the course of that crusade. The project took five years to complete, and was itself a contribution to the continuing crusade for forestry. Pointedly titling the book *Forests for the Future*, Mason wondered if anyone else would find it as interesting a subject as he did.

At least one reader of the volume referred to "the late David T. Mason," a slip that the author enjoyed immensely because he obviously continued to be very much present. Early in the 1950s, he had spent a few days in a hospital for only the second time in his life; the first stay had occurred thirty-four years before. The trouble was no more serious than appendicitis, and he discussed the operation with the surgeons as it was going on. But during that decade, death took his wife and long-time associates George Cornwall, James Girard, John Tennant, William Greeley, and Phil Weyerhaeuser. In his diary, he noted that he was the last of the original members of the O&C Advisory Board and of the Linn County Fire Association.

His longevity enabled him to accept in person honors presented to him by many organizations: the Interior Department, the American Forestry Association, the Society of American Foresters, the Oregon Historical Society, the Forest History Society, and Oregon State University. He was especially moved by a portrait by Bruce Bomberger, commissioned by the Weyerhaeuser Company, showing him surveying second-growth forestland. This testimonial, proclaiming Mason "the father of sustained-yield forestry," was reproduced in the *Saturday Evening Post* and other national magazines. In 1969 the SAF awarded him its Gifford Pinchot Medal for outstanding public service; it was

presented, appropriately, by William D. Hagenstein, executive-vice
president of the Industrial Forestry Association, who was then also
president of the SAF. As it rarely comes to men of accomplishment,
David T. Mason was thus hailed as a "legend in his own time."[11]
He died on September 3, 1973.

A Note on Primary Sources

David T. Mason's papers at the Oregon Historical Society, Portland, consist of a personal file, a business file, and microfilm copies of his diaries (the original volumes are in the Yale University Library). The collection is presently only generally organized, not indexed, and stored in temporary containers. A most useful collection concerning Mason's life and work is the file of interviews—tape recordings made by Elwood R. Maunder for the Forest History Society, Inc., Santa Cruz, California, where they are stored. (Most of the important tapes were transcribed over several years, and several transcription methods were used. As a result, the condition of the typescripts does not always permit accurate quotation of page location.) Other Mason material is included in the inactive office file of Mason, Bruce & Girard, the consulting firm he founded in Portland, and in the archives of several professional organizations, such as the Society of American Foresters also held by the Forest History Society. Important correspondence between Mason and his associates and letters about him are also located in the large collection of George Frederick Jewett Papers at the University of Idaho, Moscow.

Mason's involvement in the problems of the lumber industry is documented in the correspondence of the executive officers of the Weyerhaeuser Company, Record Group 3, in the corporate archives, Federal Way, Washington. (The boxes were renumbered after research for this study began.) The operations of west coast forest owners are exemplified in the Booth-Kelly Lumber Company Papers, Georgia-Pacific Museum, Portland (for the early twentieth century), and in the Merrill & Ring Lumber Company Papers at the University of Washington Library, Seattle (for the middle years of that period). The industry's trade associations' activities are the subject of the Industrial Forestry Association records, Portland; the National Forest Products Association (formerly National Lumber Manufacturers Association) Papers at the Forest History Society; the West Coast Lumbermen's Association Papers and the Western Forestry and Conservation Association Papers, both at the Oregon Historical Society; the Pacific Northwest Logging Association Papers, University of Washington Library; and the Western Pine Association Papers, University of Oregon Library. Two personal collections, those of William C. Reugnitz at the University of Wahington Library and Edward P. Stamm at the Oregon Historical Society, contain excellent material related to the industry's organizations. The Regional Oral History Office of the Bancroft Library, University of California, Berkeley, has the transcripts of numerous interviews on the themes of forestry, lumbering, and government.

The relationship between the lumber industry and the federal government for the period of the Timber Conservation Board, the Lumber Code Authority, and the O&C and Sustained Yield acts is also documented in the Herbert C. Hoover Papers, Hoover Library, West Branch, Iowa, the Franklin D. Roosevelt Papers, Roosevelt Library, Hyde Park, New York, and in Record Groups 9 (National Recovery Administration), 48 (General Land Office, Interior Department), and 187 (Natural Resources Planning Board), National Archives, Washington, D.C., and 95 (Forest Service, Department of Agriculture) Federal Records Center, Seattle.

The political context for the creation of federal legislative and administrative authorities in forestry is further described in the Charles L. McNary Papers, Library of Congress, Washington, D.C., the Walter H. Horning Papers, Walter M. Pierce Papers, Robert W. Sawyer Papers, Wayne L. Morse Papers, and Richard L. Neuberger Papers, all at the University of Oregon Library.

Printed primary sources for this study, including government documents, lumber trade journals, and regional newspapers, are in the collections of the Library of Congress, the University of Washington's College of Forest Resources Library, the Governors' File of the Oregon State Archives, Salem, the Forest History Society Library, and the Portland City Library.

Abbreviations Used in the Notes

Dixon/P - Algernon C. Dixon Papers,
Georgia-Pacific Museum, Portland
DTM - David T. Mason
DTM/D - David T. Mason's diaries,
microfilm copies, Oregon Historical
Society, Portland
DTM/M - David T. Mason's interviews
with Elwood R. Maunder, transcripts
of tapes, Forest History Society
Library, Santa Cruz, California
FDR/L - Franklin D. Roosevelt Library,
Hyde Park, New York
FHS/L - Forest History Society Library,
Santa Cruz, California
Graves/P - Henry S. Graves Papers, Yale
University Library, New Haven,
Connecticut
Hoover/L - Herbert Hoover Library,
West Branch, Iowa
Horning/P - Walter H. Horning Papers,
University of Oregon Library, Eugene
IFA/P - Industrial Forestry Association
Office Files, Portland
Jewett/P - George Frederick Jewett
Papers, University of Idaho Library,
Moscow
McNary/P - Charles L. McNary Papers,
Library of Congress, Washington, D.C.
M/P - David T. Mason Papers, Oregon
Historical Society Library, Portland
M-R/P - Merrill & Ring Lumber
Company Papers, University of
Washington Library, Seattle
NFPA/P - National Forest Products
Association Papers, Forest History
Society Library, Santa Cruz, California
NRA - National Recovery Administra-
tion
OHS - Oregon Historical Society,
Portland

PNWLA/P - Pacific Northwest Loggers
Association Papers, University of
Washington Library, Seattle
Pierce/P - Walter M. Pierce Papers,
University of Oregon Library, Eugene
RG 9 - Records of the National
Recovery Administration, National
Archives, Washington, D.C.
RG 48 - Records of the General Land
Office, Department of the Interior,
National Archives, Washington, D.C.
RG 95 - Records of the Forest Service,
Federal Records Center, Seattle,
Washington
RG 187 - Records of the National
Resources Planning Board, National
Archives, Washington, D.C.
Reugnitz/P - William C. Reugnitz Papers,
University of Washington Library,
Seattle
ROHO - Regional Oral History Office,
Bancroft Library, University of
California, Berkeley
SAF/P - Society of American Foresters
Papers, Forest History Society,
Santa Cruz, California
UO/L - University of Oregon Library,
Eugene
W/A - Record Group 3, Weyerhaeuser
Company Archives,
Tacoma, Washington
WCLA/P - West Coast Lumbermen's
Association Papers, Oregon Historical
Society, Portland
WFCA/P - Western Forestry and
Conservation Association Papers,
Oregon Historical Society, Portland
WPA/P - Western Pine Association
Papers, University of Oregon
Library, Eugene

Notes

INTRODUCTION

¹Paul E. Bruns, "The Philosophy and Techniques of Sustained Yield Planning in Forestry" (Ph.D. dissertation, University of Washington, 1956); Max Rothkugel, "Forest Management of Southern Pines," *Forestry Quarterly* (March 1907), 1-10; Karl W. Woodward, "The Application of Scientific Management to Forestry," *Forestry Quarterly* (March 1912), 407-416; H.H. Chapman, "A Method of Investigating Yields Per Acre in Many Sized Stands," *Forestry Quarterly* (March 1912), 458-469; Jay P Kinney, *The Development of Forest Law in America* (New York, 1917), and *Indian Forest and Range* (Washington, D.C., 1950); David T. Mason, "What is Sustained Yield to a Logmaniac?" *Logging Handbook*, volume 5 (1945), 68-71; Philip Wakeley, "Sustained Yield Management of New York State Forests" (M.A. thesis, Cornell University, 1925).

²William Heritage to DTM, January 5, 1953, 5-53, Personal, M/P.

³Wilson M. Compton, interview with Elwood R. Maunder, October 29, 1965, 108, FHS/L.

⁴Thornton T. Munger to C.L. Billings, November 14, 1930, 27, SAF/P.

⁵DTM/M, July 26, 1967, II, 19, FHS/L.

ONE

¹DTM/M, October 11, 1973.

²DTM/M, October 12, 1973.

³DTM to his parents, July 23, 1905, 3-12, Personal, M/P; DTM to James W. Girard, May 4, 1933, A-F Business, M/P; *Chronicle* (Bound Brook, New Jersey), July 28, 1905, copy, Mason, Bruce & Girard, inactive office file, Portland, Oregon.

⁴DTM/D, 1908; DTM/M, October 4, 12-15, 1965, May 24, August 11, 1966, July 15, 1973.

⁵DTM/D, 1908-1909; DTM/M, October 4, 12-15, 1965, May 24, August 11, 1966, July 15, 1973; DTM to F.E. Weyerhaeuser, February 17, 1928, 326, Business, M/P.

⁶DTM/D, 1910-1911; *Daily Missoulan* (Missoula, Montana), January 4, 29, 1909, copy, Mason, Bruce & Girard, inactive office file; *Early Days in the Forest Service*, volume 3 (Missoula, Montana: USDA-Forest Service, 1962), 165-178, 183-203.

⁷DTM/D, 1912-1915; DTM/M, October 4, 12-15, 1965, May 24, August 11, 1966, July 5, 1973.

⁸W/A, *passim*.

[9]DTM/D, 1912; WFCA, "The Situation of the Forest Industry from the View Point of Permanent Forest Management," March 1916, 8, Thomas H. Gill Papers, FHS/L; George S. Long, "What Should Lumbermen Do with the World's Greatest Market?" June 26, 1914, Henry S. Graves, report, November 1913, 171-8, M-R/P.

[10]DTM/D, 1912-1915; DTM/M, October 4, 12-15, 1965, May 24, August 11, 1966, July 15, 1973; DTM, "Utilization and Management of Lodgepole Pine," 1915, 5-30, Personal, M/P.

[11]DTM/D, 1915-1916; DTM/M, October 12-15, 1965, August 5, 6, 1966, July 15, 1973; DTM, "A California Forest Policy," 1916, "Timber Ownership and Lumber Production in the Inland Empire," 1920, Business, M/P.

[12]DTM/D, 1916-1918.

[13]DTM/D, 1919-1920, esp. May-July, October 1920; DTM/M, October 12-15, 1965, August 5, 6, 1966, July 15, 1973; DTM, "New Timber Regulations," 1920, "Forest Industries Schedules," 1921, 5-36, Personal, M/P; *American Lumberman* (September 25, 1920), 5; Circulars 2848, 2869, 171-8, M-R/P.

[14]DTM/D, November 30, December 17, 18, 1920; DTM/M, May 25, July 26, 1967, October 11, 1965, August 5, 6, 1966; F.E. Olmsted, "The Year's Accomplishments," *Journal of Forestry* (February 1920), 93-97.

[15]William B. Greeley, "Self-Government in Forestry," Burt P. Kirkland, "Co-operation between National Forests and Adjacent Private Lands," *Journal of Forestry* (February 1920), 103-105,120-130.

[16]DTM, "Comments on the Report . . .," *Journal of Forestry* (March 1920), 232-233, address, December 19, 1920, 6, WCLA/P.

[17]DTM/D, 1920-1921; *American Lumberman* (September 25, 1920), 53; DTM/M, July 15, 1973.

[18]Profile of DTM is based in part upon Wilson M. Compton, interview with Elwood R. Maunder, October 29, 1965, 22, FHS/L; Thomas J. Vaughan to the author, September 5, 1980; author's interviews with DTM's former partners, Lucien Alexander and Gilbert Bowe, November 12, 1979, with DTM's former secretary, Dorothy Patterson, November 14, 1979, and with IFA's former executive vice-president, William D. Hagenstein, December 12, 1979, FHS/L.

TWO

[1]DTM/D, 1919-1921, esp. April 19-20, 28, 1921; DTM/M, May 2, 24-27, August 5, 7, 9, 12, l966, July 16, 1973.

[2]DTM/D, 1921-1924, esp. August 20, December 15, 1921, May 10, 1924; DTM/M, May 2, 24-27, August 5, 7, 9, 12, 1966, July 16, 1973.

[3]DTM/D, August 1, October 28, 1921, March 24-26, 1923; DTM, "Permanent Forest Management for Western Timber Operators," 1921, "General Report on Redwood Forest Operations . . .," 1922, Sustained Yield, Etc., Business, M/P.

[4]DTM/D, August 26, December 28, 1921; DTM to George S. Long, September 1, 1921, Long to DTM, September 5, 1924, January 12, 1925, DTM to commissioner, General Land Office, August 4, 1922, 326, Business, M/P; DTM/D, March 14, 1928.

[5]DTM/D, January 12-14, 1922, 1925-1926; DTM to Donald MacDonald, August 5, 1925, E.T. Clark and James W. Girard to John C. Merriam and John Emmett, August 11, 1926, Sustained Yield, Etc., Business, M/P; DTM, "A Recomendation for . . . State Park Policy . . .," *Portland City Club Bulletin* (January 3, 1930), Portland Library; DTM/D, December 20, 1928.

[6]DTM/D, 1923-1924, esp. March 5, 10, 19, 28, September 3, November 26, 1923; DTM/M, August 4, 1966.

[7]DTM/D, esp. August 5, 18, September 13, 1925, April 1, 2, 8, 9, 1928; DTM, "Progress of Private Reforestation . . .," *Lumber World Review* (December 10, 1923), 27; DTM to H.W. Jackson, May 1923, 1-12, Business, M/P.

[8]DTM/D, 1923-1926; DTM/M, July 26, 29, 1967.

[9]F.E. Weyerhaeuser-C.S. Chapman correspondence, 1925-1930, 1-A, W/A; George F. Jewett-WFCA correspondence, Business, Jewett/P.

[10]U.S. Forest Service, "Outline . . .," May 1, 1912, A.F. Potter to district foresters, April 11, 1914, E.E. Carter to district foresters, May 19, 1920, "Report on the Forest Management Conference . . .," October 30- November 4, 1922, "Management Plans . . .," May 1, 1923, S. Plans, Timber Management, Weldon Heyburn to Forest Chief, Region 6, August 3, 1934, 54135, Olympic, William B. Greeley, "How Shall We Secure Reforestation?" E.N. Kavanaugh to Greeley, December 31, 1920, S. Legislation, 59854, RG 95.

[11]Carl M. Stevens to J.J. Donovan, May 19, 1926, Donovan to Stevens, May 21, 1926, 303, F.E. Weyerhaeuser to Stevens, December 1, 1925, January 7, 1926, 326, Business, M/P.

[12]DTM/D, 1927, esp. February 11, 15, 16, 18, March 4, 5, May 20-29, 1927; DTM/M, July 26, 29, 1967, August 6, 1968.

[13]DTM/D, 1927; DTM/M, July 26, 29, 1967, August 6, 1968.

[14]DTM/D, 1927; DTM/M, July 26, 29, 1967, August 6, 1968; WFCA, Forest Management Conference, Victoria, B.C., December 6-9, 1926, Jewett/P.

[15]DTM, drafts and final versions of "Putting the Brakes on . . .," and "Sustained Yield . . .," ca. February-June 1927, address lists, Sustained Yield, Etc., Business, M/P.

THREE

[1]DTM/D, 1927; DTM/M, May 24-25, 1966, July 29, 1967; respondents' letters, April-October 1927, Q, Letter Mail, Business, DTM/P.

[2]DTM, statements, *Commonwealth Review* (October 1927), Sustained Yield, Etc., Business, DTM/P; DTM, "Sustained Yield . . .," *Journal of Forestry* (October 1927), 625-658.

[3]DTM/D, 1927-1928, esp. September 11, November 3, December 31, 1927, March 5, May 15, 17, 1928; DTM/M, July 29, 1967; William B. Greeley, notes, ca. November 1927, Sustained Yield, Etc., Business, DTM/P.

[4]DTM/D, November 14, 16-17, 22-23, 1927, January 10, November 6, 1928; DTM, "With Hoover," November 23, 1927, Sustained Yield, Etc., Business, DTM/P.

[5]DTM to Ralph Arnold, January 16, 1928, Sustained Yield, Etc., Business, DTM/P; Robert Y. Stuart to William B. Greeley, January 5, 1928, Shirley Allen to John Beatty, April 24, 1928, Stuart to Allen, July 11, 1928, "Progress Report," July 11, 1928, memo for Greeley, January 5, 1928, DTM to Allen, November 13, 26, 1928, SAF/P; Henry S. Graves, diary, August 14, 1928, 83, Graves/P; "Privately Owned Timber . . . Survey," 1928, 71, NFPA/P.

[6]DTM/D, February 15, 23, 1928, January 26, September 24, 1929; Robert Y. Stuart to DTM.

[7]DTM and Donald Bruce, "Selective Logging . . .," DTM, "Timber Supply . . .," *Timberman* (October, November 1929).

[8]Depression conditions are described in: DTM/D, 1930; DTM/M, December 1,1966; ICC Docket 26000, minutes, 1932, volumes 632-635, 13, WPA/P; minutes, August 17, 1929, 176, August 24, 1929, 178, December 7, 1929, 206, June 28, 1930, 235, WCLA/P; *Crow's Pacific Coast Lumber Digest* (August 15, 1929, August 2, December 6, 1930); Wilson M. Compton to Economic Board, July 20, 1930, 27-2, Jewett/P; William C.

Reugnitz to Isador Lubin, October 15, 1934, 3-21, Reugnitz/P.

[9]F.K. Weyerhaeuser to H.C. Hornby, to George F. Jewett, April 4, 1933, 1-C, W/A; "Pulp or Lumber—Which?" 171-11, Timothy Jerome to Albert Johnson, January 22, 1931, 84-13, William B. Greeley to John Merrill, January 2, February 27, 1930, Merrill to Greeley, January 7, 1930, 921, Wilson M. Compton to manufacturers and distributors of lumber, March 1, 1932, 92, M-R/P; Ferdinand A. Silcox to DTM, July 9, 1929, DTM to Silcox, July 18, 1929, 2-8, Personal, Alex Polson to Johnson, July 27, 1929, Carl M. Stevens to Merrill, July 13, 1929, Poe-Pol, F.L. Bell to DTM, January 24, 1931, 326, Business, M/P.

[10]DTM/D, 1930.

[11]DTM/M, July 29, 1967; DTM to William B. Greeley, November 14, December 4, 12, 1930, Un-Western, Business, DTM/P; National Timber Conservation Board, correspondence, March-November 1930, President Subject File, Hoover/L; DTM/D, November 1930.

[12]DTM/D, 1931; DTM/M, December 1, 1966, July 29, 1967; Ripley Bowman to Christopher M. Granger, December 22, 1931, SAF/P.

[13]DTM/D, 1931; DTM, "Report . . .," November 14, 1931, 98, M-R/P.

[14]T.D. Woodbury, memorandum, July 31, 1931, S. Plans, Timber Management, 54135, E.A. Sherman to regional foresters, July 11, 1931, S. Plans, Timber Management, 59854, RG 95; U.S. Forest Service, "Report on Possibilities . . .," October 30, 1931, Robert Y. Stuart to Timber Conservation Board, November 23, 1931, Timber Conservation Board, President Subject File, Hoover/L.

[15]DTM/D, 1931; DTM/M, December 1, 1966, July 29, 1967; DTM and Donald Bruce, Sustained Yield . . . (Portland, 1931), DTM to William B. Greeley, May 23, 1931, Un-Western, Wilson M. Compton to Herbert C. Hoover, July 3, 1931, Timber Conservation Board, DTM to F.E. Weyerhaeuser, July 9, 1931, 326, Business, DTM/P; DTM to Franklin Reed, June 29, 1931, Forest Policy, 69, SAF/P.

[16]DTM/D, 1931; DTM/M, December 1, 1966, July 29, 1967; Walter Peacock to DTM, June 20, 1931, A.D. Folweiler to Thomas H. Gill, October 9, 1931, 8, Thomas H. Gill Papers, FHS/L; DTM, "Report of Sustained Yield Committee Project . . .," November 17, 1931, Lee Muck, "The Status of Indian Forests in Relation to a National Program of Sustained Yield," Sustained Yield, Etc., Business, DTM/P; Ripley Bowman to DTM, July 14, 1931, DTM to Henry S. Graves, July 3, September 23, October 13, November 5, 1931, Graves to DTM, July 20, September 29, 1931, Project III, IV, VIII, W.N.Sparhawk, "Public Control of Private Forests . . .," 1930, Fred Ames, report, September 1, 1931, 39-41, Graves/P; DTM to Evelyn Mason, February 8, 11, 12, 23, 28, March 1, 5, June 9, 11, 1931, 7-12, Personal, DTM/P.

[17]DTM/D, 1932, April 15, 1933; DTM/M, December 1, 1966, July 29, 1967; E. L. Hamilton to Ferdinand A. Silcox, April 5, 1932, 326, DTM to Ripley Bowman, March 21, 1932, Timber Conservation Board, Business, DTM/P.

[18]DTM/D, 1932; DTM to Evelyn Mason, July 13, 1932, Personal, 7-13, DTM/P; Timber Conservation Board, "The Forest Situation in the United States," 1932, President Subject File, Hoover/L.

[19]Timber Conservation Board, "Conclusions and Recommendations . . . ," August 1, 1932, President Subject File, Hoover/L; Legislation, 67th-71st Congresses, 21128, RG 95.

[20]DTM/D, 1932-1933; "Program Adopted by the Western Pine Association," August, 1932; "Statement of . . . Weyerhaeuser," Timberman (August 1932), Sustained Yield, Etc., Business, DTM/P.

[21]DTM/D, January-March 1933, esp. March 4, 9, 25, 1933; E. T. Allen to WFCA, January 4, 1933, 27, Jewett/P.

FOUR

¹DTM/D, April 25-26, 1933; DTM to Evelyn Mason, May 7, 18, 1933, 7-14, Personal, M/P; DTM/M, July 26, 1967; J. P. Weyerhaeuser to F. K. Weyerhaeuser, April 22, 1933, 1-C, A. W. Clapp to J. P. Weyerhaeuser, May 13, 1933, 1-A, W/A; Edward T. Allen to Gavin McLeod, June 30, 1933, 27, Jewett/P.

²DTM/D, April-May 1933, esp. April 27, May 1-3, 24-30, 1933; DTM/M, July 26, 29-30, 1967, undated, ca. 1968; Christopher M. Granger to DTM, February 2, 1933, 29, SAF/P; William B. Greeley to DTM, March 28, 1933, 13, WCLA/P; DTM to Evelyn Mason, May 7, 31, 1933, 7-14, DTM to S. Van Fullaway, May 15, 1933, 2-30, Personal, M/P.

³DTM/D, May-June 1933, esp. May 4-9; DTM/M, July 26, 29-30, 1967; DTM, "The Lumber Code" (Yale University School of Forestry, 1933; hereinafter cited as DTM, "Lumber Code"), LCA, Business, M/P; *Timberman* (March 1933), 62, (July 1933), 7; Ward Shepard to Franklin D. Roosevelt, May 29, 1933, enclosures, Henry A. Wallace to Roosevelt, June 15, 16, 1933, Roosevelt to Wallace, June 16, 1933, printed in Edgar Nixon, *Franklin D. Roosevelt and Conservation* (Hyde Park, N.Y., 1957), I, 165-182.

⁴DTM/D, May-June 1933, esp. May 20-26, 1933; DTM/M, July 26, 29-30, 1967, undated, ca. 1968, December 1, 1969, July 17, 20, 1973; minutes, May-June, volume 238, WCLA/P; Algernon C. Dixon, "History of the Code of Fair Competition for the Lumber and Timber Products Industries: Code #9, Approved August 19, 1933" (hereinafter cited as Dixon, "History") copies in Dixon/P and in 7573, RG 9.

⁵DTM/D, June-July 1933, esp. June 3, 7, 9, 17-30, July 2, 1933; DTM/M, July 26, 29-30, 1967, December 1, 1969, July 17-20, 1973; Dixon, "History"; DTM, "Lumber Code."

⁶C. L. Hamilton to J. P. Weyerhaeuser, June 9, 1933, A. W. Clapp to Weyerhaeuser, August 4, 1933, Weyerhaeuser to Clapp, August 17, 1933, 1-A, W/A; Dixon, "History"; DTM to William C. Reugnitz, October 11, 1933, 1-49, Reugnitz/P; F. E. Weyerhaeuser to Laird S. Bell, August 12, 1933, 1-B, W/A.

⁷DTM/D, July-August 1933; DTM/M, July 26, 29-30, 1967, July 17, 20, 1973; F. E. Weyerhaeuser to A. W. Clapp, August 10, 1933, 1-B, W/A; DTM, "Lumber Code"; Dixon, "History."

⁸DTM to Evelyn Mason, May 20, 22, June 26, July 20-21, 23, November 5, 1933, 7-14, Personal, M/P; DTM statement, July 21, 1933, "Transcript of Hearings, 1933-1935 . . . " (hereinafter cited as NRA, hearings, RG 9), 87-113, 1061-1063, 7160, RG 9; F. K. Weyerhaeuser to DTM, May 31, 1933, J. P. Weyerhaeuser to F. K. Weyerhaeuser, June 1, 1933, 1-C, C. L. Hamilton to J. P. Weyerhaeuser, July 12, 1933, A. W. Clapp to J. P. Weyerhaeuser, August 4, 1933, J. P. Weyerhaeuser to Clapp, August 17, 23, 1933, 1-A, W/A; Wilson M. Compton, interview with Elwood R. Maunder, October 29, 1965, 24, FHS/L; DTM/D, July 11-15, August 1, 10-11, 17, 1933; DTM/M, July 26, 29-30, 1967, December 1, 1969, July 17, 20, 1973; Timothy Jerome to Stiles Burr, June 26, 1933, 95-23, M-R/P; NLMA, press release, ca. October 1933, Department of Agriculture, press release, October 24, 1933, Henry S. Graves, diary, September 1, 1933, Graves/P; Henry A. Wallace to Franklin D. Roosevelt, June 16, July 20, 27, November 10, 1933, printed in Nixon, *Roosevelt and Conservation*, I, 181-182, 194-196, 217.

⁹Dixon, "History"; Hugh S. Johnson, *Blue Eagle—From Egg to Earth* (New York, 1935); DTM/D, August 19-20, 24-31, 1933.

¹⁰DTM/D, September-October 1933.

¹¹*Timberman* (July 1933), 7; Wilson M. Compton to George F. Jewett, August 15, September 6, 1933, 26, Jewett/P; F. E. Weyerhaeuser to J. P. Weyerhaeuser, October 2, 1933, J. P. Weyerhaeuser to F. E. Weyerhaeuser, October 11, 1933, 1-B, W/A; DTM/D, October 21-25, December 16-31, 1933, January 3-4, 6-12, 22-29, February 26, March 7-8, 14-17, 1934; "Report, Conference . . . October, 1933, January 1934," reprinted in *Journal*

of Forestry (March 1934), 275-307; DTM to Compton, October 13, 1933, to J. P. Weyerhaeuser, November 15, 1933, to Evelyn Mason, January 27, 29, February 1, 7-14, Personal, M/P; Jewett to Edward T. Allen, September 15, 1933, DTM to Jewett, September 15, 26, 1933, Allen to Compton, August 21, 1933, Jewett to SAF, October 14, 18, 1933, J. W. Blodgett to Compton, November 4, 1933, Jewett, "An American Plan for Forestry," November 29, 1933, R. G. Hall to Jewett, January 12, 1934, 26, 27, Jewett/P; J. P. Weyerhaeuser to F. R. Titcomb, March 1, 1934, 2-A, W/A; Thornton T. Munger, interview with Amelia R. Fry, September 7, 1962, 157-160, ROHO; George L. Drake, interview with Elwood R. Maunder, 1975, FHS/L.

[12]John B. Tennant to Hugh S. Johnson, April 2, 1934, 2-17, Personal, M/P; Wilson M. Compton to Henry A. Wallace, May 26, 1934, Joint Committee, minutes, April 1934, 2, Business, M/P; Wallace to Franklin D. Roosevelt, July 20, 1933, Roosevelt to Wallace, July 27, 1933, Rexford Tugwell to Roosevelt, November 8, 1933, enclosures, printed in Nixon, *Roosevelt and Conservation*, I, 194-196, 212-216; DTM to Evelyn Mason, April 2, 1934, 7-14, Personal, "Summary . . . Legislative Program . . . , " Joint Committee, minutes, January-April 1934, 2, Business, M/P; DTM to Western Pine Association, February 24, 1934, S. Forest Code, Cooperative, S. Legislation, 59854, RG 95; Compton to Roosevelt, May 16, 1934, Roosevelt to Compton, June 13, 1934, 2-32, Personal, M/P; DTM/D, January 3, 11-12, March 30-31, April 5, 1934.

[13]Wilson M. Compton, "Problems Arising . . . ," April 15, 1934, 2-B, W/A; Lumber Code Authority, minutes, October 16-November 1, 1933 (hereinafter cited as LCA, minutes, RG 9) in 213, Reel 92, Series 21, RG 9; C. S. Chapman to W. E. Heidenger, March 12, 1934, 2-A, Laird S. Bell to J. P. Weyerhaeuser, August 22, September 16, October 26, November 9, 27, December 19, 1933, J. P. Weyerhaeuser to Bell, November 2, 1933, 1-A, F. E. Weyerhaeuser to Bell, January 3, 1934, F. K. Weyerhaeuser to F. E. Weyerhaeuser, December 1, 1936, 26, J. P. Weyerhaeuser to F. K. Weyerhaeuser, June 1, 1933, A. C. Clapp to J. P. Weyerhaeuser, August 23, November 7, 1933, 1-A, W/A; minutes, October 20, 1933, volume 165, WCLA/P; minutes, December 11, 1933, 1, PNWLA/P; *West Coast Lumberman* (March 1934), 7; *Southern Lumberman* (June 1, August 15, 1933); William B. Greeley to William C. Reugnitz, June 22, 1933, Reugnitz to LCA, October 3, 1933, Reugnitz/P; W. T. Lee to Walter M. Pierce, July 22, 1933, 10, Pierce/P; Timothy Jerome to Louis Moore, July 20, 1922, 95-24, M-R/P.

[14]Laird S. Bell to J. P. Weyerhaeuser, October 26, 1933, 1-A, W/A; DTM to Dudley Cates, February 17, 1957, 5-53, to S. Van Fullaway, May 15, 1933, 2-30, to Edgar H. Polleys, June 13, 1934, 7, Personal, M/P; *Timberman* (April 1934), 9; Wilson M. Compton, interview with Elwood R. Maunder, 109, FHS/L; Compton to C. L. Hamilton, December 1, 1933, 27, Jewett/P; F. E Weyerhaeuser to J. P. Weyerhaeuser, July 12, 1933, 1-B, J. P. Weyerhaeuser to Laird S. Bell, November 2, 27, 1933, 1-A, A. C. Clapp to J. P. Weyerhaeuser, August 23, November 7, 24, Bell to Weyerhaeuser, September 16, 1933, 1-A, W/A; LCA, minutes, October 16-November 1, 1933, RG 9; DTM, statement, NRA hearings, January 22, 1934, RG 9; DTM to Evelyn Mason, January 27, 1934, R. W. Wetmore to DTM, June 8, 1934, 2-17, Personal, M/P; DTM/D, September 1933-June 1934, esp. November 2, 1933, March 21, May 27-28, June 4, 10, 1934; J. P. Weyerhaeuser to DTM, June 13, 1934, 2-B, W/A.

FIVE

[1]DTM/D, June-October 1934; DTM/M, July 20, 29, 31, August 1, 4, 15-16, 1967; LCA minutes, January-February, June-July, September-October 1934, 312, Business, M/P.
[2]Dixon, "History."
[3]DTM/D, June-July 1934; DTM/M, July 20, 29, August 1, 4, 15-16, 1967.

[4]William C. Reugnitz to DTM, May 29, July 12, 1934, 3-20, Reugnitz/P; DTM to James G. McNary, July 6, 1939, notes, 323, Business M/P.

[5]William B. Greeley, statement, and minutes, Trustee Board, September 25, October 30, 1934, 6, WCLA/P.

[6]DTM/D, March-July 1934, esp. March 28, April 17, May 22, June 7-8, 9, 18, 30, July 4, 24, 1934; Dixon, "History"; A. W. Clapp to J. P. Weyerhaeuser, June 13, 1934, 2-A, W/A; *Timberman* (June 1934), 7.

[7]DTM/D, July 1934; DTM/M, July 20, 29, 31, August 1, 1967; Hugh S. Johnson, NRA, hearings, RG 9, 235.

[8]Charles Hardy to Algernon C. Dixon, October 12, 1934, 2, Dixon/P; Timothy Jerome to M. N. Brady, May 11, 1934, to John Moore, May 19, 1934, 102-10, M-R P; DTM to Dixon, July 2, 25, 26, August 24, 26, September 28, 1934, LCA minutes, RG 9; Dixon, "History"; DTM/M, August 15, 1967, August 3, 1968.

[9]*Timberman* (March 1934), 7; *Southern Lumberman* (December 1934), 9; Timothy Jerome to Petrus Pearson, April 4, 1934, 102-15, M-R/P; William C. Reugnitz to DTM, April 29, 1934, 3-20, Reugnitz/P.

[10]Ralph McAlin to Algernon C. Dixon, April 9, 1934, 2, Dixon P; WCLA, Trustees Board, minutes, October 20, 1933, March 16, May 16, 1934, 6, WCLA P; A. W. Clapp to J. P. Weyerhaeuser, November 3, 1934, Clapp to F. K. Weyerhaeuser, October 9, 1934, "Before the Control Committee . . . ," 2-B, W/A.

[11]WCLA, minutes, March 16, 1934, volume 221, WCLA P; Timothy Jerome to Stiles Burr, November 8, 1934, 102-10, M-R/P.

[12]*Timberman* (October 1934), 7; DTM/D, August 29, October 12, 1934; WCLA, Trustees Board, minutes, March 16, May 16, 1934, 6, WCLA P; C. H. Kreienbaum to J. W. Watzek, August 3, 1934, 2-B, W/A.

[13]DTM/M, August 15, 1967, August 3, 1968, undated, ca. 1968; E. A. Miekeljohn to Merrill & Ring Lumber Company, January 16, 1935, 112, Merrill & Ring to LCA, February 23, 1935, 110, M-R/P; C. D. Johnson to William B. Greeley, September 4, 6, 1934, 2-B, W/A; Dixon, "History"; Ralph McAlin to Algernon C. Dixon, April 9, 1935, Charles Hardy to Dixon, October 12, 1934, 2, Dixon P.

[14]DTM/M, August 15, 1967; Blackwell Smith to LCA, December 10, 1934, Bernice Lotwin to Algernon C. Dixon, December 17, 1934, Lee Robinson to DTM, December 26, 1934, Landon Bell to DTM, December 31, 1934, 2, Dixon P; LCA, minutes, June-July, September 1934, RG 9; Dixon, "History."

[15]DTM/D, June-September 1934, esp. June 24, August 14-16, 24, September 28, 29, 1934; DTM/M, July 28-31, August 1, 16, 1967; DTM to NRA, August 1, 1934, DTM to Algernon C. Dixon, September 6, 1934, DTM to Carl Bahr, September 17, 1934, Donald Richberg to DTM, October 5, 1934, Dixon to NRA, October 22, 1934, LCA, 312, Business, M/P.

[16]DTM to NRA [Leon Henderson], November 12, 1934, 7, Leon Henderson Papers, FDR/L.

[17]DTM/D, September-December 1934, esp. September 5-6, 11, 18, October 5, 6, 11, 21, November 15, 1934; Dixon, "History"; LCA, minutes, September 11, 12, 1934, RG 9; WCLA, minutes, September 25, October 30, 1934, 6, WCLA P; Wilson M. Compton to Edward T. Allen, November 20, 1934, 13, WFCA P.

[18]DTM/D, December 13, 1934, January 9, 10, 1935; DTM, statement, January 30, 1935, NRA hearings, 1255-1266, RG 9; Blackwell Smith, statement to LCA, December 10, 1934, Bernice Lotwin to Algernon C. Dixon, December 17, 1934, 2, Dixon P; Sol Rosenblatt to LCA, January 22, 1935, 312, Business, M P.

[19]DTM to LCA divisions and subdivisions, December 24, 1934, LCA, 312, Business, M/P.

[20]DTM/M, August 15, 1967; Edward Polleys to DTM, December 12, 1934, January 17, 1935, 8-1, Personal, M/P; LCA, minutes, January 1935, RG 9; DTM to LCA divisions

and subdivisions, January 3, 23, 1935, 312, Business, M/P; Algernon C. Dixon to H. J. Cox, January 16, 1935, 2, Dixon/P; Dixon, "History"; "Survey of the Effect of Suspension of Prices," January 12, 1935, DTM, memorandum on Blackwell Smith, February 8, 1935, WCLA, minutes, October 30, 1934, 6, WCLA/P; PNWLA, minutes, February 10, 1935, 1, PNWLA/P.

[21]DTM, "Lumber Code"; DTM, statements, January 30, February 2, 1935, Donald R. Richberg, statements, March 26, 31, 1935, "Questions Put to . . . Rosenblatt," March 30, 1935, 312, Business, M/P.

[22]DTM/D, February 28, 1935; DTM/M, February 28, March 28-29, August 1, 4, 7, 15, 16, 1967, undated, ca. 1968.

[23]George McNulty to John Grisson, February 19, 1935, 312, Business, M/P; Donald R. Richberg, *The Rainbow* (New York, 1936), 215-216, 219; Thomas Vadrey, *Wayward Liberal* (Lexington, Ky., 1970), 162-163.

[24]Max Freedman, *Roosevelt and Frankfurter: Their Correspondence, 1928-1945* (Boston, 1967), 259-260; Richberg, *Rainbow*, 219; Department of Justice, press release, March 25, 1935, 13567, Series 49, RG 9.

[25]DTM/D, March 22-25, 1935; Wilson M. Compton, "Meaning of *Belcher* Case Dismissal," Compton, "Comments on Code Situation," March 29, 1935, 312, Business, M/P; *Southern Lumberman* (April 1, 1935), 19.

[26]DTM/D, March 26, 28, 29, 1935; DTM, "Survey of Wires Received," March 29, 1935, 312, Business, M/P; WCLA, minutes, March 29, 1935, 6, WCLA/P.

[27]DTM/D, March 26, April 1, 1935; Donald R. Richberg to Franklin D. Roosevelt, April 3, 1935, OF 466, FDR/L; Wilson M. Compton to John B. Tennant, April 1, 1935, 312, Business, M/P.

[28]New York *Times*, March 30, 1935, cited in DTM/D, March 30; LCA, minutes, March 30, 31, April 1, 9, 1935, 312, Business, M/P; Richberg, *Rainbow*, 219.

[29]DTM/D, March 6, 13, 20-22, 28-29, April 9, 1935; WCLA, minutes, May 9, 1935, volume 221, 6, WCLA/P; Cornelius Lombardi to DTM, April 1, 1935, DTM to Lombardi, April 16, June 1, 1935; LCA minutes, April 9, 1935, RG 9; Timothy Jerome to Stiles Burr, April 9, 1935, 109-18, M-R/P; DTM to William C. Reugnitz, April 1, 1935, 3-21, Reugnitz/P.

[30]DTM/D, April-May 1935, esp. April 9, 11, 1935; DTM to Carl Bahr, May 12, 1935, 312, Wilson Compton, "Comments on the Code Situation," March 29, 1935, 326, Business, M/P; Compton to Ferdinand A. Silcox, April 10, 1935, 2, Dixon/P.

[31]DTM/D, April 15-18, 26, May 1-3, 1935; DTM/M, April 15, 1967; Dixon, "History"; DTM, statement, exhibits 5-40, DTM to LCA divisions and subdivisions, May 27, 28, June 6, 1935, 312, Business, M/P; DTM to William C. Reugnitz, 1-49, Reugnitz/P; DTM to Dudley Cates, February 17, 1953, 5-53, Personal, M/P.

[32]DTM/D, May 27-29, June 2-5, 10-14, 18-24, 1935; DTM to LCA divisions and subdivisions, June 6, 1935, RG 9; Carl Bahr to DTM, July 9, 1935, 312, Business, M/P.

SIX

[1]DTM/D, October-December 1935, esp. November 22, 1935; William B. Greeley to R. D. Merrill, May 4, 1935, 112, M-R/P; J. P. Weyerhaeuser to F. E. Weyerhaeuser, February 26, 1935, 3-B, "Report of Forest Management Committee . . . ," November 15, 1934, J. P. Weyerhaeuser to J. Titcomb, December 10, 1934, 2-B, W/A; DTM to Robert Rosenbluth, February 6, 1960, 2-6, Personal, M/P; Carl M. Stevens to J. P. Weyerhaeuser, April 1, 1935, 326, Business, M/P.

[2]Laird S. Bell to J. P. Weyerhaeuser, December 14, 20, 1935, enclosure, 1-A, C. S. Chapman to W. E. Heidinger, May 17, 1934, J. P. Weyerhaeuser to F. R. Titcomb, March

1, 1934, 2-A, W/A; DTM, "Summary of . . . Forest Protection . . . ," ca. November 1934, 2-32, "Meeting of . . . Joint Committee . . . ," November 1934, 2-35, Personal, M/P; LCA, minutes, November 28, December 14, 1934, RG 9.

³DTM to A. B. Recknagel, November 14, 1934, to Evelyn Mason, January 22, 1935, 7-15, Personal, M/P; DTM/D, March 12, 1935; Franklin Reed to H. H. Chapman, August 3, 1934, 47, SAF/P; PNWLA, minutes, April 14, 1934, X, 13, PNWLA/P; Ferdinand A. Silcox to regional foresters, Portland, September 15, 1934, S. Plans, 54135, RG 95; F. H. Brundage, "Organization and Management of Sustained Yield Units," October 3, November 2, 1934, B. Frank Heintzelman to regional foresters, April 15, 1934, C. J. Buck to LCA, February 16, 1934, S. Plans, Timber, 54135, RG 95.

⁴Franklin D. Roosevelt to state governors, January 2, 1935, Rexford G. Tugwell to Roosevelt, January 8, 1935, Tugwell to Marvin H. McIntyre, June 19, July 1, 1935, McIntyre to DTM, June 15, 1945, printed in Nixon, *Roosevelt and Conservation*, I, 339-340, 383-384; Ferdinand A. Silcox, "Forestry—A Public and Private Responsibility," January 28, 1935, 10, Pierce/P; C. S. Martin to John B. Woods, January 23, 1935, 21, NFPA/P; DTM to Julian Rothberg, January 23, 1935, 2-5, Personal, M/P; Carl M. Stevens to J. P. Weyerhaeuser, April 1, 1935, Stevens to Silcox, April 1, 1935, 3-B, W/A; DTM to Silcox, March 2, 1935, 2-32, Personal, M/P.

⁵DTM to Ferdinand A. Silcox, March 2, 1935, 2-32, Personal, M/P; Franklin D. Roosevelt to Duncan U. Fletcher, March 30, 1935, Marvin H. McIntyre to DTM, June 19, 1935, DTM to A. B. Recknagel, May 31, 1935, 2-32, Personal, M/P; "Forest Restoration Bill," Foreign Relations, 64, NFPA/P; C. J. Buck to Silcox, April 1, 1935, S. Legislation, 59854, RG 95; George F. Jewett, "The Return of Forest Ownership to Liberty," ca. April, 1935, 28, Jewett to Silcox, June 2, 1936, 30, Jewett/P.

⁶Stuart Moir to H. H. Chapman, April 16, 1935, 1-A, SAF/P; George F. Jewett to C. L. Hamilton, January 14, 1935, Hamilton to Jewett, January 4, 1935, 28, Jewett to A. G. Moore, July 18, 1936, 30, John B. Woods to Jewett, February 21, 1935, Jewett to Wilson M. Compton, September 20, November 27, 1935, Jewett to Duncan U. Fletcher, July 11, 1935, E. T. Allen to Jewett, February 21, May 5, June 21, 1935, 29, Allen to Compton, February 22, 1935, 28, Jewett/P; Allen to Jewett, May 17, 1936, 31, WFCA/P.

⁷DTM/D, June-September 1935, February-March 1936, esp. June 19, August 7, September 26, October 24, 25, November 1, 6, December 21, 31, 1935, January 22, February 9, 1936; DTM to A. S. Murphy, August 25, 1935, Sustained Yield, Etc., Business, M/P; "Report of the Pacific Northwest Regional Planning Conference," February 13-15, 1936, Oregon State Planning Board, "Oregon's Forest Problems," 1936, 4, Edward P. Stamm Papers, OHS; Laird S. Bell to J. P. Weyerhaeuser, August 21, 1935, J. P. Weyerhaeuser to A. W. Clapp, September 27, 1935, F. E. Weyerhaeuser to G. L. Berry, October 29, 1935, 3-A, W/A.

⁸DTM to Ferdinand A. Silcox, March 31, 1936, DTM, notes, ca. April-May, August 1935, April-May 1936, Sustained Yield, Etc., Business, M/P; John B. Woods to DTM, February 17, 1936, 2-34, Personal, M/P.

⁹DTM/D, February-April 1936; DTM/M, August 6-7, 1969; DTM, notes, ca. April 1936, 2-21, Personal, M/P; DTM to Evelyn Mason, April 15, 1936, 7-15, Personal, M/P; C. J. Buck to Ferdinand A. Silcox, October 8, 1935, S. Legislation, 59854, RG 95; William B. Greeley, "Comments on the McNary-Doxey Bill," December 7, 1936, 21, NFPA/P; DTM, "Relationship of Forestry to the . . . Region," February 14, 1936, Marshall Dana to DTM, April 14, May 20, 1936, Dana to Pacific Northwest Planning Commission, April 23, 1936, DTM to Dana, May 20, 1936, 42, RG 187; C. S. Chapman, report, Conference of Public Agencies, H. J. Cox to Charles L. McNary, February 3, 1934, 39, Charles W. Eliot to McNary, January 9, 1930, Guy Cordon to McNary, December 24, 1934, John B. Woods to DTM, March 11, 1936, George Gerlinger to

Woods, April 8, 1936, 39, Woods to Harold L. Ickes, May 13, May 25, 1936, 42, McNary/P.

¹⁰The voluminous sources documenting the origins, drafting, and passage of the O&C Act of 1937 are in Elmo Richardson, *BLM'S Billion-Dollar Checkerboard: Managing the O&C Lands* (Washington, D.C., 1980), 185; DTM/D, May-July 1936, esp. May 5, June 16, July 9, 24, 27, 1936; DTM/M, August 4, 1968; Ward Shepard to Harold L. Ickes, February 26, 1934, 1-70/3, RG 48; George Gerlinger to John B. Woods, April 8, 14, 1936, 42, Woods to Ickes, May 23, 1936, 39, McNary/P; DTM to J. P. Weyerhaeuser, April 17, May 12, 1936, 4-13, Personal, C. C. Shepard to DTM, May 28, June 17, 326, Business, DTM to Evelyn Mason, May 15, 1936, 2-34, Personal, DTM to Ferdinand A. Silcox, November 27, 1936, OC-FS, M/P.

¹¹DTM/D, May-July 1936, esp. May 5, June 16, 1936; DTM to Evelyn Mason, May 7, 1936, 7-15, Personal, M/P; DTM to J. P. Weyerhaeuser, May 12, 1936, 4-B, W/A.

¹²DTM/D, July 24, 27, 1936; Harold L. Ickes to Henry A. Wallace, et al., July 6, 1936, "Minutes of a Meeting of . . . the Oregon State Planning Board," July 24, 1936, 3196, RG 48.

¹³DTM/D, July-November 1936, esp. July 27, November 13, 1936; "Hearings . . . ," July 27, 1936, 3196, RG 48; DTM to Merrill & Ring Lumber Company, September 8, 1936, 116-19, M-R/P.

¹⁴DTM/D, November 1936-August 1937, esp. March 31, April 2, 8, 13, August 21, 1937; Ward Shepard to Rufus Poole, December 1, 1936, Solicitor's File, RG 48; DTM to Ferdinand A. Silcox, November 27, 1936, C. S. Martin to Edward T. Allen, September 25, 1936, DTM to John B. Tennant, December 12, 1936, DTM, statement, "Hearings . . . O&C Bill . . . ," April 13, 1937, A-For, Un-West, Business, M/P.

¹⁵DTM to Rufus Poole, August 28, 1937, 2-3, Personal, M/P; DTM/D, December 8, 27, 1937; DTM to Poole, November 29, 1936, to Lee Muck, December 11, 13, 1937, Poole to E. K. Burlew, November 16, 1937, Solicitor's File, RG 48; Walter H. Horning to Poole, October 17, 1936, to Harold L. Ickes, November 16, 1937, 2, Horning/P.

¹⁶Walter H. Horning to Shirley W. Allen, February 2, 1938, 2, Horning/P; DTM/D, 1938-1944, esp, July 13, 26, August 28, 1938, December 16, 1941, September 22, 1942; O&C Advisory Board, minutes, 1938-1944, Mason, Bruce & Girard, inactive office file, Portland; DTM to Percy Pratt, December 17, 1941, 4259, RG 48; DTM/D, December 1, 1936, September 14, 1937; DTM to Julius Hult, September 17, 1937, June 2, September 15, December 19, 1939, notes, September 1934, 308, Business, M/P; Richard S. Kearns to Horning, September 19, 1940, 1, Horning, "Planning Sustained Yield . . . " 1942, 2, Horning/P; DTM to Joel Wolfsohn, February 26, 1944, Un-West, Business, M/P.

SEVEN

¹Jewett to A. G. Moore, July 18, 1936, 30, Pacific Logging Congress, "Status of National Forestry Programs," October 7, 1936, 13, Jewett/P; William B. Greeley, "Survey of Experiences . . . ," December 19, 1939; Frederick L. Jewett to Ward Shepard, August 28, 1940, 64, NFPA/P.

²DTM/D, 1938, esp. March 14, 16, 1938; DTM to Roy Bessey, August 10, 1938, 75, RG 187; DTM to George F. Jewett, April 28, 1938, Jewett to C. S. Martin, August 5, 1938, 33, Jewett/P; DTM to J. P. Weyerhaeuser, February 3, 1938, Weyerhaeuser to DTM, February 13, 1938, 326, Business, M/P; DTM to Florence Wolfe, July 2, 1938, 75, Bessey to DTM, September 16, December 29, 1938, DTM to Bessey, August 10, December 30, 1938, 74, RG 187.

³Fred Brundage to Ferdinand A. Silcox, November 20, 1937, Silcox to C. J. Buck, December 1, 1937, S. Legislation, 59854, RG 95; Silcox to E. H. O'Neil, June 6, 1939, 4l, W/A.

⁴DTM to George F. Jewett, June 22, 1938, 17, Jewett/P; Warren G. Tilton to John B. Woods, January 5, 1938, H. J. Cox to James G. McNary, January 3, 1938, 2, NFPA/P; DTM to Ferdinand A. Silcox, February 1, 1939, A-For, Business, M/P; DTM to Charles Boyce, August 11, 1938, 500-51, Boyce to DTM, September 1, 1938, A-B, NFPA/P.

⁵Jewett to J. J. Farrill, July 5, 1938, to C. S. Martin, August 5, 1938, 5, DTM to Jewett, November 1, 16, 1939, 34,5 Jewett/P; DTM/D, December 12, 13, 1939; DTM to J. P. Weyerhaeuser, July 28, 1938, 15, F. E. Weyerhaeuser to J. P. Weyerhaeuser, April 19, 1938, 16, Laird S. Bell to J. P. Weyerhaeuser, March 29, 1939, J. P. Weyerhaeuser to Bell, April 13, 1939, 41, memorandum for F. E. Weyerhaeuser, August 16, 1939, 18, W/A.

⁶R. A. Scott, correspondence, February 25, March 8, 28, 1939, Personal, Frank Bryan to Page Bettner, February 6, 1941, Forest Conservation, Portland Chamber of Commerce Archives.

⁷DTM/D, 1939, esp. January 9, March 23, April 14, 1939.

⁸DTM/D, January 23, 1941.

⁹Laird S. Bell to George F. Jewett, March 29, 1939, 41, Jewett/P; G. H. Collingwood, memorandum, August 14, 1941, 2, NFPA/P; DTM/M, July 29, 1967, February 2, 1969; DTM, notes, March 31, 1937, A-For, DTM to Warren G. Tilton, April 28, 1938, William B. Greeley to Tilton, May 8, 1939, Un-West, M/P; DTM to Charles L. McNary, January 18, 1938, 39, McNary/P.

¹⁰Marshall Dana to Duncan U. Fletcher, April 14, 1936, 5, RG 187; William B. Greeley to Gifford Pinchot, September 30, 1939, 7, William B. Greeley Papers, UO/L; J. P. Weyerhaeuser to C. S. Martin, January 11, 1943, 40, W/A; Seattle *Post-Intelligencer*, September 15, 1940; Martin to Warren G. Tilton, April 17, 1940.

¹¹DTM/D, November 20, December 23, 1942, January 14, 15, 1943; DTM/M, February 2, 1968; John B. Woods to William B. Greeley, February 13, 1941, G. H. Collingwood to James G. McNary, April 23, 1941, 21, NFPA/P; DTM to A. W. Clapp, February 9, 1940, A-For, 323, Business, M/P; Collingwood to C. S. Chapman, May 7, 1941, DTM to Collingwood, April 21, 1941, DTM to McNary, August 22, 1941, McNary to DTM, August 26, 1941, Collingwood to files, August 14, 1941, McNary to J. P. Weyerhaeuser, January 13, 1942, 40, W/A; DTM to E. D. Smith, January 20, 1943, Charles L. McNary to Smith, January 20, 1943, 39, McNary/P.

¹²DTM/D, 1943, esp. February-March, May, July, September, October, December; DTM/M, July 29, 1967, February 2, 1968; DTM, notes, December 17, 1942, DTM to George F. Jewett, February 28, March 14, May 2, 27, July 9, November 17, 1943, to H. J. Cox, July 23, 1943, to G. H. Collingwood, December 13, 22, 1943, Collingwood to DTM, March 23, 1943, Nels Rogers to Collingwood, December 2, 1943, 40, Jewett/P; DTM to MacDonald Denman, July 13, 1943, to Charles Hines, July 27, 1943, 710-11, Business, DTM to Evelyn Mason, January 17, February 8, 13, March 7, April 20, July 5, October 16, 21, 1943, 7-16, Personal, M/P.

¹³DTM/D, January-March, 1944; DTM to Evelyn Mason, January 27, March 3-4, 16, 21, 1944, 7-16, Personal, M/P; DTM to M. Harris Ellsworth, February 25, 1944, 4, M. Harris Ellsworth Papers, UO/L; George F. Jewett to DTM, March 23, 1944, Collingwood to DTM, March 1, 23, 1944, 40, Jewett/P; Helen Kiefer to Guy Cordon, March 22, 1944, 39, McNary/P; DTM to Jewett, March 25, 1944, 21, NFPA/P.

¹⁴DTM/D, 1944-1946; DTM to James G. McNary, April 16, May 23, 1944, to Christopher M. Granger, May 8, 1944, 710-4, McNary to DTM, June 8, 1944, Un-West, Business, M/P; DTM to F. B. Lenzie, July 25, 1945, to Robert W. Sawyer, January 10, 1946, Sawyer to Guy Cordon, August 1, 1945, Cordon to Sawyer, August 7, 1945, 8, Robert W. Sawyer Papers, UO/L.

¹⁵DTM/D, March 18-19, April, June 7, 1937, February 2, September 22, 1938, April 14, 27, 1939, May 14, September 14, 30, 1940, June 28, 1941, February 22, December 12, 1942, April 19, 1944, June 22, 27, 1945; DTM/M, August 6, 11, 1966, August 6, 1968,

May 2, April 30, 1969; Gilbert Bowe of Mason, Bruce & Girard, Portland, to the author, January 3, 1980; Bowe, interview with the author, November 12, 1979; H. J. Andrews to DTM, July 6, 1945, Acting Regional Forester to Charles L. Tebbe, June 3, 1945, S. Plans, Cooperative, 10898, RG 95.

[16]Sources documenting the Interior Department's proposed Siuslaw Unit are in Richardson, *BLM's Billion-Dollar Checkerboard*, 187-188; *Oregonian* (Portland), November 11, 1945; "Analysis of Testimony . . . ," December 3, 1945, 260, Land Utilization, RG 48; H. C. Hall to G. H. Collingwood, April 8, 1944, Wellington Burt to Collingwood, April 8, 1944, Collingwood to DTM, August 28, 1944, 21, NFPA/P; DTM/D, February 14, 1946.

[17]DTM to Guy Cordon, March 6, 1946, 11.623, IFA/P; DTM/D, 1946, esp. February-March, July 1946; "The Cooperative . . . Situation," February 8, 1946, 21, NFPA/P; DTM to Roy Morse, August 20, 1946, to Guy Cordon, July 20, 1946, 710-11, James W. Girard to George Gerlinger, June 4, 1946, T-Z, Business, M/P; Gerlinger to Cordon, March 8, 1946, 11.623, IFA/P; "The Promise of Industrial Forestry," June 25, 1946, WCLA/P; Walter H. Horning, "Now the Public Can Be Told," July 9, 1946, C. S. Martin to DTM, February 25, 1946, 11.326, IFA/P.

[18]Wellington Burt to G. H. Collingwood, April 8, 1944, 21, NFPA/P; Collingwood to DTM, May 28, 1944, 710-11, Business, M/P; DTM/D, May 23, 29, June 4, September 15, 1946, March 12, 27, 1947; William B. Greeley to Walter Tilley, November 26, 1943, 11.623, IFA/P; J. C. Stevens to Henry Fowler, February 1, June 28, 1946, 1, WCLA/P; George L. Drake, interview with Elwood R. Maunder, 1975, FHS/L; H. J. Andrews to Lyle F. Watts, December 31, 1946, S. Plans, Cooperative, 10897, RG 95, C. H. Kreienbaum, interview with Elwood R. Maunder, 1972, FHS/L; Edmund Hayes to J. P. Weyerhaeuser, August 30, 1946, 40, C. S. Martin to Weyerhaeuser, September 5, 1946, Minot Davis to Weyerhaeuser, September 6, 1941, 41, Laird S. Bell to Weyerhaeuser, October 9, 1946, 36, W/A. For the establishment of the Simpson Unit see: Roy O. Hoover, "Public Law 273 Comes to Shelton: Implementing the Sustained-Yield Forest Management Act of 1944," *Journal of Forest History* (April 1978), 86-101.

EIGHT

[1]DTM/D, 1947-1948, esp. June 7, 17, July 21, August 15, September, 1947; sources documenting the history of the proposed Mohawk cooperative sustained yield unit are listed in Richardson, *BLM's Billion-Dollar Checkerboard*, 187-188.

[2]Walter H. Horning, "The Promised Land . . . ," October 1947, S. Plans, Cooperative, 10897, RG 95; DTM/D, 1948-1949, esp. January-June, 1949; DTM/M, August 4, 1966; DTM to George Hays, March 19, 1947, to Wayne L. Morse, October 23, 1947, February 16, 1948, David McLean to Morse, October 23, 1947, Hays to John B. Tennant, January 24, February 13, 1948, DTM to Richard S. Kearns and Horning, January 20, 1948, and enclosure, DTM to F. W. Powers, April 18, 1948, DTM to Robert W. Sawyer, April 8, 1948, Kearns to George W. Peavy, May 21, 1948, Sustained Yield, Etc., DTM, notes, February 1947, 323, Business, M/P.

[3]Daniel Goldy, interview with the author, December 10, 1979, FHS/L; DTM/D, June-October, 1948; Forest Conservation, Inc., minutes, March 2, 1950, A-For, M/P; Richard S. Kearns to George W. Peavy, July 10, 1948, Wayne L. Morse, "Brief in Support . . . ," DTM to Samuel T. Dana, August 17, 1948, 10-11, Personal, DTM, statement, Interior Committee hearings, September 7-10, 1948, 486-502, Sustained Yield, Etc., Business, M/P.

[4]DTM/D, 1948-1952, esp. September 7, 9, October 8, November 4, 5, 12, 16, 19, 1948, April 16, June 24, 1951; DTM/M, August 6, 1968; DTM to C. H. Kreienbaum,

November 23, 1948, She-Saw, 323, to C. Girard Davidson, December 14, 1948, C. D. Johnson folder, M/P.

[5]Laird S. Bell to F. K. Weyerhaeuser, October 24, 1949, 62, W/A; "In Public Hearings . . . ," 1952, Lloyd Olson to Industrial Forestry Association, June 6, 1952, Jack Heintzelman, "Five Year Review . . . ," December 23, 1954, FS, "Forest News," February 21, 1952, 11.613, IFA/P.

[6]Stuart Moir to DTM, June 23, 1949, William D. Hagenstein to WCLA et al., July 27, 1949, M. Harris Ellsworth to DTM, July 18, 1949, DTM to Herbrt C. Berkes, July 18, 1949, to C. H. Watzek, June 30, 1949, to Guy Cordon, June 29, 1949, L-B, C. D. Johnson folder, M/P; D. J. Kilpatrick to files, March 11, June 23, 1949, S. Plans, Cooperative, 10898, RG 95.

[7]F. K. Weyerhaeuser to John F. Reedy, March 3, 1953, Forestry-Federal, 78, W/A; Richard E. McArdle, interview with Elwood R. Maunder, March 1975, FHS/L.

[8]Jack Heintzelman, "Five Year Review . . . ," December 23, 1954, Walter Lund to William D. Hagenstein, April 25, 1955, "Proposed Wind River Unit . . . ,"1955, A. Z. Nelson to Federal Association, June 6, 1957, T. D. Morse to James Murray, May 29, 1957, Chrysogonus H. Kreienbaum to Hagenstein, March 3, 1958, "Brief of Simpson . . . in Opposition to Repeal . . . ," 1958, 11.613, IFA/P.

[9]N. E. Bjorklund, executive vice-president, Industrial Forestry Association, interview with the author, June 16, 1980, FHS/L; Weyerhaeuser Timber Company, "Private Forestry in the West," Western Pine Association, "Report . . . ," 1952, 73, W/A; Thomas C. Adams, "Cooperative and Federal Sustained Yield Forest Units—A Problem to Recover Management" (Ph.D. dissertation, University of Michigan, 1952); DTM/D, March 16, November, 1949.

[10]DTM to Charles A. Sprague, February 6, 1959, 2-8, to Wes Ullman, January 3, 1963, to Wilbur Mills, March 22, 1972, 2-15, Personal, M/P.

[11]DTM's final years are documented in: DTM/D, 1952-1957, esp. November 22, 1952, November 14, 1953, August 20, 1957; Rodney C. Loehr, *Forests for the Future: The Story of Sustained Yield as Told in the Diaries and Papers of David T. Mason* (St. Paul, Minn., 1952), 15-16; *Saturday Evening Post, US News and World Report*, July 1956. The portrait is now at OHS, a copy accompanies DTM, "Memoirs of a Forester . . . ," *Forest History* (January 1967; the remainder of the article appears in that journal's issue for April/July 1969).

Index